the ESCAPE PLAN

a 40-DAY PLAN to ANNIHILATE the ADULTITIS in YOUR LIFE

the ESCAPE PLAN

by Kim and Jason Kotecki

JBiRD iNK, Ltd.
Madison, Wisconsin

This book is dedicated to our parents, who gave us the priceless treasure of a wonderful childhood and continue to support us in all our crazy endeavors.

Far too many people think that forgetting what it is like to think and feel and touch and smell and taste and see and hear like a three-year-old means being grownup. When I'm with these people I, like the kids, feel that if this is what it means to be a grownup, then I don't ever want to be one.

Madeleine L'Engle, A Circle of Quiet

Acknowledgements

Special thanks to all of the people who have joined us in this project, especially the ones who played guinea pig at the very beginning. Alex, Doug, Ian, Jaimie, Jenna, Katie, Marci, Marisa, Sue, Walt... this book would be much skinnier and less interesting without you.

BEWARE OF MIDGETS IN DISGUISE!

Table of Contents

Introduction

We want to rid the world of Adultitis. We can't afford to set up a research team to develop a vaccine. We don't have the stamina to attempt a triathalon to raise funds. And when it comes to those little ribbons, all of the colors have already been taken. But we do have a plan.

We're not sure when it happened. We thought we were fine. And because we never thought it would happen to us, it was easy to miss the warning signs. But before long, it became clear: we were afflicted with Adultitis.

Adultitis is a silent epidemic that has been ignored for far too long. It's a disease that slowly erodes our inborn childlike spirit, wreaking havoc on our world, our nation, and our families. It kills laughter, dreams, curiosity, faith, happiness, and hope. It stresses us out. It causes us to take ourselves too seriously. And in some extreme cases, it can cause smile amnesia. (Pretty serious stuff.)

Disgusted with the condition we found ourselves in, we wondered if it was possible to systematically turn the tide on Adultitis. After much soul searching and many long discussions late into the night, we developed The Escape Plan. Using Jason's book (*Escape Adulthood: 8 Secrets from Childhood for the Stressed-Out Grown-Up*) as a starting point, we wanted to create something that would be structured, yet personal and unique to each person who tries it. We wanted it to be a real-world solution, which is why it doesn't advocate that you pay your bills with Monopoly® money, take up a strict diet of chicken nuggets, or quit your job to mess around with Play-Doh® all day. That's childish. The Escape Plan is about becoming more child*like*. It's about re-programming our grown-up selves to see life through a different lens.

The Escape Plan started as a very public experiment, and we volunteered ourselves as the guinea pigs. Every day, we individually completed each challenge and posted the results on our web site. Visitors were invited to not only participate in the challenges, but also vote on who did a better – and more creative – job of capturing the spirit of childhood. Kim edged Jason in the voting, but we were happy to see that The Escape Plan produced an outcome of real and lasting change in both of our lives. We made the decision to turn The Escape Plan into a journal in order to reach more people and provide an outlet for them to record their thoughts in a more permanent fashion. This book includes our insights and solutions to each challenge as well as excerpts from other folks who have partici- pated in The Escape Plan.

Adultitis leaves its victims in shackles, weighing them down with stress and anxiety while keeping them from the simple peace and joy they had as children. We envision The Escape Plan to be like a key, designed to unlock our minds and free our spirits.

It's pretty simple, really: The Escape Plan is a 40-day journey. Each day brings with it a challenge de- signed to get you thinking and acting in a more childlike way. We recommend that you record your daily experiences and personal observations in this journal as you go along. We also invite you to share your solutions and experiences for each challenge in the comment section of each blog post at www.EscapePlanBlog.com. Your input will make the experience that much richer for everyone else who follows you on this journey.

This project is quite challenging. All change is. But it's also a TON of fun. Why not try the Plan and see what happens?

About Kim...

"Kim is my wife. My biggest supporter. My best friend. And a noodle-aholic. Her infectious childlike spirit was the first thing that attracted me to her. She retired from teaching kindergarten in order to help out with our company, a.k.a. our dream. (I call her a 'retired' teacher, which sounds funny to me – and probably no one else – because she's only in her 20s.) Kim has always been as close to Adultitis-free as anyone I know, but I sense that the pressures that have come with running a business without much of a safety net is responsible for opening the door to Adultitis. I'm looking forward to seeing how she tackles each challenge, and expecting to learn a lot from her through this process."

*–Jason on Kim, 01/02/06 (Read Kim & Jason's blog at **www.EscapeAdulthood.com**)*

About Jason...

"Jason is a five-year-old trapped in an adult's life. As a dreamer and a man of incredible faith, these two characteristics have given Jason what's he's needed to start and persevere in our business. Jason inspires me to be a better me. Between his art, design, writing, and speaking talents, his passion and creativity are mind-boggling. He loves to read, loves his Macs, and proudly wears his many superhero shirts. His childhood dream of being a superhero has become real in his incredible drive to save adults from Adultitis and in protecting the childhood of little ones who are at risk of growing up too fast. Every superhero has their own version of 'kryptonite.' Jason's often involves the worries and stress related to taking the necessary risks involved in running a business. I think these next 40 days will help him defeat the threats that every superhero faces."

*–Kim on Jason, 01/02/06 (Read Kim & Jason's blog at **www.EscapeAdulthood.com**)*

ADULTITIS

It has wrought an epidemic of stress, anxiousness, and depression. It has plundered laughter. It has transformed people into zobmie-like doo-doo heads. It all ends here. The Escape Plan is dedicated to increasing awareness while providing diagnosis and treatment for Adultitis, the sinister epidemic that makes the Black Death look like a trip to Disneyland.

What exactly is Adultitis?

Adultitis is a common condition occurring in people between the ages of 21-121, marked by chronic dullness, mild depression, moderate to extremely high stress levels, a general fear of change, and, in some extreme cases, the inability to smile. Patients can appear aimless, discontent, and anxious about many things. Onset can be accelerated by an excess burden of bills, overwhelming responsibilities, or a boring work life. Generally, individuals in this condition are not fun to be around.

How many people have Adultitis?

Unfortunately, because it often goes undiagnosed, there is no way to tell how many people are currently living with Adultitis. If we had to put a number on it, based on our current research, we'd have to say... a lot. It's certainly an epidemic. So whatever number it takes to qualify as an epidemic, multiply that by at least three. In comparison, Adultitis makes the Black Death plague of 1347 look like a trip to Disneyland.

Who discovered Adultitis?

Although Adultitis has been around for centuries, it has only recently been discovered and named by Jason Kotecki. The first breakthrough came when he made the peculiar observation that children rarely complain about being stressed and seem to enjoy life way more than grown-ups. Further research unveiled that the average four-year-old laughs over 400 times a day, while the average adult laughs just 15 times per day. He found that this discrepancy between children and grown-ups was not caused simply by a decrease in exposure to Saturday morning cartoons and knock-knock jokes, but by a real, debilitating disease he ultimately dubbed Adultitis.

Is Adultitis lethal? What are the effects of Adultitis?

Yes, Adultitis can kill you. Adultitis causes stress – lots of it. And stress has been linked to all of the things that kill us, from heart attacks to cirrhosis, suicide to accidents. In fact, 75% of all of our doctor visits are stress-related. People who are relatively Adultitis-free tend to live much longer, enjoy life much more, and are less likely to have co-workers and family members go out of their way to avoid them. Adultitis not only causes stress, but it can be responsible for a loss of vitality, sleeplessness, anxiety, and in some extreme cases, the complete inability to smile. Obviously, it's a force to be reckoned with.

How does a person contract Adultitis?

There are many different ways in which a person can contract Adultitis. Here are a few known ways:

- *By being in close proximity to others with Adultitis for extended periods of time.*
- *By sticking with a job that makes you want to poke your eyes out with chopsticks, regardless of how much money you make.*
- *By ignoring your dreams to pursue the things that your mom/neighbor/society thinks you should do.*
- *By regularly answering, "Because we've always done them this way" whenever someone asks, "Why do we do things this way?"*
- *By constantly chasing the "next big thing" and consciously or subconsciously or trying to "keep up with the Joneses."*
- *By habitually taking oneself too seriously, while neglecting things that make you smile.*
- *By becoming a slave to what other people think, and masking your true identity from others.*
- *By engaging in a perpetual deluge of activities that keep you busier than a one-armed busboy working at Applebee's on a Saturday night.*
- *Finally, some studies show that people who don't believe in a higher power have a much higher risk of contracting Adultitis.*

Can Adultitis be cured?

It is rare for Adultitis to be completely cured, but it can happen. Typically, Adultitis is treated and brought into a controllable state of remission. Of course, the earlier Adultitis is detected in an individual, the easier it is to treat and control. With a steady, non-intrusive and ongoing treatment plan, most people can live productive, exhilarating, and relatively Adultitis-free lives.

Why is Adultitis often undiagnosed?

Adultitis goes undiagnosed for a variety of reasons. For one, adults are not usually able to discern whether or not someone has Adultitis simply by looking at him or her. (Ironically, children can spot an adult with Adultitis almost immediately.) Secondly, most of the physicians who are in position to diagnose and treat patients often have Adultitis themselves, which at best clouds their judgment or in worst-case scenarios, causes them to deny Adultitis even exists. Finally, up until now, we really knew very little about Adultitis. That is why it is so important that you get yourself tested, and help spread awareness to others.

Do You Have Adultitis?

Complete the following intake to find out if you have Adultitis. Answer the questions as honestly as you can. If you think more than one applies to you, just try to pick the one that fits best.

#1 On any given weekend, I'm more likely to be found:

a) doing chores around the house.
b) working, what else?
c) playing a sport or enjoying a hobby.
d) attending a boring family obligation.

#2 My desk/work space predominantly features:

a) office supplies, neatly arranged.
b) an assortment of unique toys and mementos.
c) a stack of papers a mile high.
d) a bulletin board with photos of loved ones.

#3 This is what I think about following dreams:

a) My dreams are so big, I think most people think I'm mental.
b) I don't really have time for my dreams.
c) Three words: Get. A. Job. People should spend more time with their feet on the ground than heads in the clouds.
d) I do have dreams, but I try to keep them realistic.

#4 When I go to the zoo, I'm more likely to notice:

a) the outrageous price of a Coke. And the souvenirs. And don't get me started on the selfish crowds.
b) my watch. We've got a lot of stuff to cover and I want to see it all.
c) the amazing variety and colors of animals, and how everything works together just so.
d) the name animals. You know, things like elephants, lions, tigers, and bears.

#5 During my lunch break on a beautiful spring day I'd be most likely to:

a) take a really quick walk.
b) stay at my desk--there's too much to do.
c) sit outside and read over some paperwork.
d) take the rest of the day off and go somewhere fun.

#6 During conversations, when someone brings up something I'm not very familiar with:

a) I'll quickly change the conversation.
b) I pretend I know exactly what they're talking about -- who wants to look like an idiot?
c) I'll ask them more about it right then and there.
d) I'll try and find out more about it later.

#7 When a child dances in front of my cart at the grocery store, I'm most likely to:

a) smile, wink, and wave.
b) wonder why parents can't keep their kids under control.
c) yell at her to move it or lose it -- I'm in a hurry!
d) ignore her and wait for her to move.

#8 Children are:

a) awfully cute, but best when quiet.
b) my role models.
c) little guides who have wisdom that I often overlook.
d) those annoying things that spill stuff, get in your way, and scream on airplanes.

#9 If I was at a formal dinner and someone noticed some toilet paper stuck to my shoe, I'd:

a) immediately leave the room and avoid that person for the rest of my life.
b) subtly kick it off and act like it was no big deal.
c) remove the toilet paper and suggest that whoever is in charge of keeping the restrooms clean should be fired.
d) smile and say, 'I guess it never hurts to have some extra on hand.'

#10 If I had to compare the excitement level of my life to a type of animal, it would most likely resemble:

a) a peacock. Colorful and often quite breathtaking.
b) a tortoise. Kind of slow, but I keep myself busy.
c) a dead tortoise.
d) a penguin. Active, but I'm not exactly flying, you know? (Which is pretty similar to everybody else I know.)

#11 I would estimate that I laugh approximately:

a) 5-10 times a day.
b) 10-20 times a day.
c) way too many times a day to count.
d) How am I supposed to laugh with the whole world going to pot?

#12 When my alarm goes off in the morning, I typically:

a) groan, hit the snooze button and bury my head under the pillow.
b) smile and jump out of bed.
c) sit up, yawn, and contemplate my day.
d) throw my freakin' alarm out the window.

Answer Key

	a	b	c	d
Question #1	a=2	b=4	c=1	d=3
Question #2	a=3	b=1	c=4	d=2
Question #3	a=1	b=3	c=4	d=2
Question #4	a=4	b=3	c=1	d=2
Question #5	a=3	b=4	c=2	d=1
Question #6	a=3	b=4	c=1	d=2
Question #7	a=1	b=3	c=4	d=2
Question #8	a=3	b=1	c=2	d=4
Question #9	a=3	b=2	c=4	d=1
Question #10	a=1	b=3	c=4	d=2
Question #11	a=2	b=3	c=1	d=4
Question #12	a=3	b=1	c=2	d=4

Diagnosis

12-20 points: Negative. Congratulations, you are Adultitis free! You are able to easily recognize Adultitis in others. If you know someone who you think might have Adultitis, read further to see what stage your friend might be in and what you can do to help. As far as this book goes, you really don't need it (but you'll still find it to be quite fun). You could always pass it along to someone who needs it more.

21-29 points: Stage 1 Adultitis. We don't want to alarm you, but you have a mild case of Adultitis. You may be experiencing fits of chronic dullness and occasional cases of the blahs. This book will help you get into tip top shape.

30-39 points: Stage 2 Adultitis. You have progressed to a very aggressive form of Adultitis. You are probably experiencing very high stress levels and may be having difficulty laughing. Begin The Escape Plan now. Repeat as needed.

40-48 points: Full-blown Adultitis. This is really serious. Your life is spiraling out of control and people no longer enjoy being around you. Don't despair, there is hope. Besides undertaking The Escape Challenge immediately, consult the additional information starting on page 187 for advanced treatment instructions.

Challenge #1:

Different World

For kids, every day is a new adventure, with new things to see, learn, and explore. As we get older, our well of experience increases, our curiosity dwindles, and we settle into familiar comfort zones. Eventually, these comfort zones turn into ruts. We stop growing, and vitality is sucked from our lives. By taking some time to explore areas in which we are unfamiliar, we can wake up our brains and bring back a little intrigue into our lives. Additionally, we are providing our brain with new experiences that it can use to make new connections to help us solve problems.

The Challenge: Spend at least 15 minutes immersing yourself in a field you know nothing about.

Kim:

It was made obvious to me after a near-death experience on a recent trip to Milwaukee that I would like to learn more about cars. As we were on the side of the snowy road with car problems, I faced the humbling fact that I wasn't quite sure how to even open the hood of our Pontiac. "Our hood is tricky," I rationalized. This is embarrassing for me to admit but a harsh reality.

So, I sat down with a "Fix It Yourself" book from Reader's Digest and some very helpful web sites (about.com and howstuffworks.com) and spent my fifteen minutes learning Car Parts 101. Fifteen minutes was not nearly enough. I am still curious about the other parts under the hood that I didn't get to. I really only got through the basics of how the car uses the gasoline to accelerate and the chain of command that happens with the parts in this procedure. Combustion, cooling, pistons, exhaust... lots of familiar words that are now clearer with some handy dandy animations. This challenge shined the light on my "perfectionist" side that gets too overwhelmed and is often fearful to learn something new. It forced me to become curious and take the risk of looking foolish. Kids just naturally ask hundreds of "why" questions and they are learning new things every day. It is good to be reminded of that feeling. It was fun!

Jason:

Today I immersed myself in an alien world right out of a *Star Wars* movie (at least to me): an oriental grocery store. I know from watching those behind the scenes *Star Wars* documentaries that the artists take great efforts to create each planet from scratch, with its own native language, look, and culture. After only a few moments in Lee's Oriental, surrounded by produce I've never seen and labels with words I couldn't read, I half-expected to hear George Lucas step out from behind the aisle saying, "And, cut."

I started checking out the jars and jars of sauces: peanuts, soy, and whatnot. Then I came across an interesting package that seemed out of place. The product inside was almost black, and it looked like a small folded Hobbit blanket. It said "dried laver" on the label. Before I could finish asking myself the question, "What's dried laver?" I noticed another similarly stuffed package with the subhead "seaweed." Cool.

The three shelving units in the crowded store were a feast for the senses: packages of dried anchovies, broiled ferns, and lots of cans of lychees (not sure what those were but they looked like skinned eyeballs). I almost laughed out loud when I saw, amidst the exotic jars of pickled this and dried that, a few cans of Spam® (perhaps the most inedible thing in stock, in my estimation).

I scanned a spinner of packaged snacks, delighted to find an assortment of dried squid, right above bags of party mix. The squid reminded me of beef jerky — chicken jerky, I suppose — and the back of the bag touted it as "a great on-the-go snack and perfect for parties." Indeed!

On my way out of the store, I came across a row of giant bags stacked near the wall. "They sell potting soil in oriental grocery stores?" I asked myself. "Must be for rare, hard-to-maintain Asian flowers," I answered confidently.

Upon further inspection, I learned that they were actually bags of rice. It made perfect sense, of course, but I couldn't help but fancy the idea of my mom trying to jam a 10 pound bag of rice in the pantry next to the pancake mix and egg noodles. All in all, a pretty neat 15 minutes. Now, if you don't mind, I need to go find out what lychees are.

- -

Alex:

I decided to tackle The Escape Plan challenge, and for #1 I thought I'd learn about the world of phonetics. I have a slight speech impediment, so I thought it'd be interesting to learn about something that relates to speech. What was meant to be fifteen minutes of reading turned into just over an hour.
Now I know what epethensis (inserting a vowel, consonant or syllable into a word to aid pronunciation e.g. "um-buh-rel-la"), elision (the opposite of epenthesis e.g. "O'er"), non-rhotic (the letter "R" only pronounced when followed by a vowel e.g. "red" but not "water"), glottal stop (the sound made when the vocal chords are pressed together e.g. the sound in-between "uh" and "oh" in "uh-oh") and oxytone (the stressed last syllable of a word e.g. "correct") mean. I also tried to learn a bit of the phonetic alphabet, but that'll take more than a day! I know this will probably seem extremely boring to some people, but hey, it intrigued me.

Sue:

Well, today I decided to learn about ice skating. I'd love to learn how to do that someday and considering that all I know about it is that it looks pretty, I thought I could learn a thing or two. So, some of the first things I learned concerned me a little, like: "Skills to learn: How to fall," "Make sure you have medical clearance," "Try not to fall on your hands," and "Keep your hands from being hurt by other skaters' blades." (Ok, now I'm a little concerned.) I realize there's a whole lot to learn about just standing up on skates, let alone actually moving and not dying. Needless to say, I have a lot of respect for people who can actually skate. I wanna think it's just like roller skating in the 1980s and although some techniques might be similar, I think this is a little more dangerous. I have to go consult my doctor for medical clearance now.

Instaparty

Little things are big deals to kids, and they don't need an invitation to celebrate them. Whether it's losing a tooth, the first snowfall of the year, finding a penny on the ground, or discovering two marshmallows joined together in their Lucky Charms,® these are all perfectly acceptable grounds for celebration. We grown-ups allow ourselves specific days to celebrate – Christmas, birthdays, anniversaries – but too often the tasks associated with planning these events can dissolve much of the spontaneous fun and joy.

The Challenge: Find a reason to celebrate and do something to celebrate it.

Kim:

Happy 1st Hump Day (for 2006, that is)! In my opinion kids are experts at celebrating. They don't need any official notice from Hallmark® for permission to celebrate. They know what it takes to make for a fulfilling celebration. Typically the components are as follows: special "eats," decorations or hats, and games.

I did the best I could with the resources I had, which I think is key to this challenge. Please don't go out and buy a bunch of stuff. I found some fun camel clip art online and printed off a few copies. I also dug out the camel from our Christmas nativity set. I hung up a few pictures of camels and prominently displayed the camel figurine on a shelf with some white Christmas lights. Bringing in the celebratory eating, I made camel-shaped pancakes for breakfast and a carrot cake, drawing a camel on the top, for dessert. Oh yes, and my camel hat, which I made from the clip art pictures.

I proudly wore my hat to the zoo to make a special visit to today's mascot. Not only am I lucky enough to have a free zoo two miles from my house, but both of the camels were out and happy to have a visitor on this cold, dark day.

My game of choice for this special occasion: pin the hump on the camel. Jason spun me way more than I spun him, leaving me quite "off." Being a retired kindergarten teacher gave me a slight advantage. From losing a tooth to the 100th day of school – you name it, we celebrated it! The camel pancakes were fun but nothing beats green eggs for breakfast on Dr. Seuss' birthday.

Jason:

I was a little under the weather today. But not so much so that I couldn't celebrate Earth at Perihelion Day. That's right folks, today is the one day that the Earth is as close to the sun as it will be all year. The holiday is surprisingly absent from my calendar and there is a glaring omission in the online catalog of Hallmark® eCards (perhaps a Kim & Jason greeting card is in order…)

I must admit that Earth at Perihelion Day is not a holiday I'm accustomed to celebrating, so I wasn't quite sure how to correctly mark the occasion. I assumed that we were headed for a hot spell,* so I got decked out in my swimming trunks, Cruisin' for Wishes t-shirt, and sandals (this little detail really had Kim smiling, as I NEVER wear sandals). My accessories included an authentic plastic Hawaiian lei, some beads I got once at Red Lobster, and a jester hat. I'm not sure where the jester hat fits in, but it IS festive, and Earth at Perihelion Day is nothing if not festive.

All in all, it has been a great day. A simple, fun holiday, free from the trappings and commercialization of corporate giants like Hallmark. For now.

*As later research indicated, this was an ill-conceived assumption.

Doug and Katie:

Well, the thing we celebrated today was "Second Hand Wardrobe Day." In honor of this occasion, we went through the closet and found some clothes that either we didn't wear or didn't fit. Then Doug and I took a nice drive (to celebrate Mr. Chrysler inventing his first car today) to the Goodwill. We dropped off the clothes and did some shopping of our own. It was a great way to give back and celebrate as well.

Parker:

Celebrated mud. Went on a mud run and found every puddle possible (not hard in Seattle), the muddier the better. Got some good looks at the office when I walked back in after the excursion.

Jenna:

January 5th is National Bird Day and I decided to celebrate my favorite bird - PENGUINS! After waking up under my penguin sheets, I put on my penguin t-shirt, drank my coffee from my penguin mug and filled my Chilly Willy water bottle.

The best part of my celebration was sharing some tiny penguin stickers at the bank, the gas station, work, and even the post office. In fact that's my favorite story of the day...

After waiting in a super long line with 15 other folks for one of two overworked post office staff members, it was my turn. As my packages were being stamped, I was sharing my celebration with the helpful worker. She thanked me for the laughter. Before I left, I offered her a tiny penguin sticker - she immediately stuck it to her shirt. As I was walking away, I heard her say to the next person in line, "She gave me a tiny penguin sticker, what do *you* have for me?"

I smiled and celebrated another aspect of the day - bringing happiness to another person. That's worth celebrating and I think I'll keep a sheet of those tiny penguin stickers with me and see who else I can celebrate life with and maybe laugh just a bit.

Challenge #3:

Says You

Where is it written that kids get to have all the fun? Why do we have to say goodbye to some of the things we loved to do as children, just because the calendar tells us we're older? The sad fact is that most of us spend way too much time worrying about what other people think. We are big fans of a statement that goes something like this: "When I was twenty, I worried about what other people thought of me. When I was forty, I stopped caring about what other people thought of me. Now that I'm sixty, I've realized that nobody was thinking about me at all." There's a lot of truth in that statement, and it should serve as a reminder to worry less about what "other people" think.

The Challenge: Do something that is typically seen as inappropriate for someone your age.

Kim:

One thing that I loved about childhood that I wish would be appropriate in adulthood is the act of building blanket forts. Having older sisters, I was introduced to this activity pretty early on. Then, all of a sudden you get a little too big to be under there. I remember when I would babysit in junior high and high school, I often suggested the "blanket fort" as an option for something to pass the time. The kids loved it, as most kids do.

Having a workspace at home gave me a huge advantage with this one. No cube neighbors
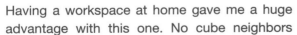
would give me strange looks. I grabbed some tacks, rubber bands, and an old sheet (a blanket would've been too heavy to rig up as tall as I needed it to be). My actual workspace is pretty small and it pretty much fit under my propped-up sheet, a.k.a. "cool fort." It did invoke a childlike excitement sitting under there, typing away and making calls. If only the person on the other end could see me — oh my, this WAS inappropriate for someone my age.

Jason:

I spent a lot of time thinking about this one. I was feeling a bit over-matched by Kim's Hump Day extravaganza yesterday — camel pancakes?! As soon as I began thinking about this challenge, I knew what I wanted to do, but it didn't seem big enough. I tried to come up with something larger than life, showy, a big production. Try as I might to come up with something really daring, I kept coming back to these two words: Happy Meal.®

When I was a kid, we hardly ever got McDonald's Happy Meals. With three boys, it was always cheaper for my parents to buy us each a cheeseburger and have us split a large fry. But oh how I pined for those Happy Meals. The colorful little boxes, printed with messages of untold joy, hinting at the wonderful toy hidden inside. (Sadly, most of the boxes have been replaced by less than exhilarating paper bags — kids of today don't even know what they're missing!) I can probably count on one hand how many Happy Meals I have had in my lifetime, and I'm guessing it has been over twenty years since my last one.

I thought about the irony: when I was a kid, I wanted Happy Meals but couldn't do anything about it; now that I'm a "grown-up," I could get a Happy Meal any time I want, but might be considered a freak job ordering one without the cover of a small child nearby.

Well that fear of being labeled a social outcast ended today, my friends, as I proudly stepped to the counter to order my cheeseburger Happy Meal.

And what a Happy Meal it was.

- -

Walt:

Tonight my wife Linda and I went to a very nice restaurant in our town called John's North Star. I complimented our waitress Connie about her very nice snowman pin and said, "I would like a kiddie cocktail in your fanciest glass, please."

When I got home, I did three Bugs Bunny dot-to-dot sheets and topped that off with coloring a picture in my Bullwinkle coloring book. I broke the brown, had a hard time staying in the lines, and was troubled by the color scheme.

Marisa:

While I often do things seen as typically inappropriate for someone my age, I think I even surprised myself today when, during downtime in the courtroom, I suggested a Karaoke Party (still celebrating from yesterday's challenge?) and, in honor of Wilson Pickett, sang *Mustang Sally* a capella. We'll see if the judge (I'm an attorney in, of all places, juvenile court) allows me in the courtroom on Monday! I almost had him sold on Karaoke Fridays…

Sue:

Today I skipped and sang *Skip to My Lou, My Darlin'* outside, in front of a very large department store - the IKEA® in the north suburbs of Chicago. Then I proceed to skip (albeit slowly) through the revolving glass doors with two people in the same compartment as me. It was kinda fun!

Challenge #4:
Souvenir From Childhood

In order to get ourselves thinking and acting in a more childlike way, it's important that we invite our inner child to come out and play. One way of doing this is to bring more reminders – triggers, if you will – into our daily lives. These little tokens will not only deliver more smiles to our day-to-day lives, but they'll inspire the people we live and work with to lighten up and drop their guard a bit too, resulting in more honest, fun, and rewarding relationships.

The Challenge: Add something childlike (not necessarily childish) to your workspace or home.

Kim:

A few months ago I read the book *Fish*, which inspired me to make my space more playful. I spent a Sunday afternoon while Jason was watching football adding fun pictures, quotes, and toys to my workspace. Because I feel pretty good about the childlike feel of my office, I wanted to add something more intangible. Having Adultitis often leaves me with frustrating side effects. Maybe you experience them as well: worry, doubt, pessimism, and fatigue. Even though I want to have that childlike joy and hope which shines from every childhood picture of myself, it doesn't always come naturally. It would be hard to put childlike joy and hope on my shelf, but I can try to consciously do things that help me live with passion and have a better perspective on things.

So I made a "Joyful Hope" container, in which I will put little notes of things that give me hope and bring me joy as a grown-up. On those days in which I need to be reminded of these childlike Adultitis-free qualities, I will take out one of the small, folded up pieces of paper and hopefully be inspired to change my attitude and actions. The first thing that I wrote down was the hope I felt seeing the sun shine today after two weeks of clouds.

Jason:

Creatively, this may have been the trickiest one yet. My office space — and most of our home, for that matter — looks like it was decorated by Geoffrey the Giraffe of Toys R Us® fame. My office is always

a highlight for kids, a veritable smorgasbord that includes Spiderman action figures, a cardboard cutout of Boba Fett (wearing a jester hat and lobster beads), Play-Doh® containers, a few Beanie Babies®, a Slinky®, an alligator head from Florida, a lava lamp, and an abundance of other toys too numerous to count.

Needless to say, adding another item of childhood whimsy to this hodgepodge would be like tossing a fistful of sand into the Mojave Desert. So I was forced to think outside the box, which led me inside a box. The ice box, as my grandma would say; the refrigerator, in 21st century terms.

So I took my Larry the Cucumber squeeze toy and squeezed him between the lemon juice and French dressing. He seems to like it there. Who knew opening the refrigerator could be so much fun?

Alex:
I play Star Wars Miniatures, and because I have quite a few I usually keep them in boxes until the next game. Well, for Challenge #4, I took all of them out and placed them on top of my desk things (printer, hi-fi, and so on). They look quite nice on there, actually.

Marci:
For this challenge, I created an "Escape Adulthood" playlist on my iPod with all kinds of fun childlike themed songs. Songs from my favorite Disney® movies, Veggie Tales®, and other fun songs like Go Fish's *Ladybug* song. I can enjoy this little bit of childhood at home, at work, or anywhere in between!

Ian:

This one prompted me to just do something simple but nice. I went into the garden and grabbed a handful of daffodils, a hydrangea flower, and leaf, and the head of an agapanthus. I put these into a bowl, arranged them nicely, and then set them on the table.

Jen thought it looked nice, and it seemed like a very childlike thing to do. Flowers are beautiful, and these aren't your normal flower arrangement type. Beautiful.

Walt:

At first I thought this would be a tough one. Anyone that knows me knows that I am a child at heart and I have a lot of Snoopy® stuff, die cast cars, trains of all types, and Kim & Jason® stuff at home and on my desk at work.

So I decided to go at this one from a different angle. I went in the old toy box in the basement and I picked out about twelve small toys. Then I went down to my lumberyard after hours and placed these toys at each of my co-workers' desks. My boss Pete always wanted to learn to fly so he got a pilot. Bill raises mules so he got a tiny mule. Ray is called "Technoman" so he got a little robot. Joe deer hunts so he got a very, very tiny deer. To try to throw them off, I put something on my desk. I can't wait until Monday morning when my co-workers discover their new desk partner!

[Update on Challenge #4: Placing little toys on my co-workers' desks was a huge success! There was a buzz around the office as each person found his or her little treasure. What a way to start a Monday morning! All fingers pointed to me but I came back with the point that I also got a surprise, so there! As I was placing the surprises on the employees' desks Saturday night, I decided to place our newest employee's surprise *in* her desk. Everyone was very excited as one by one each person came out with the surprise. And with every happy announcement it made the new girl, Patty, sadder and sadder. She was really disappointed that everyone got something except her. Her co-workers looked around and on her desk, but nothing. Then someone suggested she should look in her desk and there it was. She screamed in excitement when she found a little girl in a toy car with a clear dome in the back and a tiny rabbit running around in a circle through a tunnel. I think she felt she got the best surprise of all. As they tried to figure this mystery out, one called the other the "Toy Bandit." I plan on telling Pete because with his pilot I hope to encourage him to take flying lessons.]

Challenge #5:

Mad Scientist

A toddler who sticks everything she can get her hands on in her mouth and a three-year-old who squirts an entire tube of toothpaste into dad's shoe are essentially doing the same thing: experimenting. They're exploring the world around them, gathering data, and figuring out how things work. Experimenting is not just for kids and research scientists. Let your curiosity be your guide. You may be surprised at what breakthroughs you discover. At the very least, you'll have a little fun and be able to bask in the rewarding feeling of a curiosity satisfied.

The Challenge: Become a scientist. Conduct a silly experiment.

Kim:

This challenge gave me permission to try something I've been curious about. So many times I am too concerned about looking silly as an adult. Why do I take myself so seriously? My curiosity led me to ask: "Will bubbles freeze mid-air outside if the temperature is below freezing?" My childlike logic hypothesized that, "Yes, indeed, they would freeze. If rain fell, it would freeze, so why not bubbles?" I was so excited to see frozen bubbles.

Well, I was wrong. They did not freeze. It was 29 degrees, just below freezing. I am still curious if the outcome would be different on a day when the temperature is 0 or below. I'll keep you posted, as I can guarantee that we will soon have a day that cold in Wisconsin.

Jason:

One marble. A glass of water. How long would it take my wife to realize that the marble was in her glass of water? The experiment began at 1:38 p.m. Pacific Standard Time and concluded at 2:04 p.m.. Approximately 26 minutes.

And it was HI-larious.

Doug and Katie:

Today we conducted an experiment with the help of Mapquest®. We always wondered if the distance and estimated time Mapquest gives out would be correct. So tonight we set off to get some good eats from Little Caesars®. Before we left, we got the information we needed from the internet and we were off. Mapquest said it would take a total of 8 minutes and 5.43 miles and actually it was a perfect match! We were surprised. Now, this little experiment worked for a small distance, but we will see on longer ones another time.

Marisa:

My experiment was to see if boxer briefs really are more comfortable than boxers. Having never worn either with jeans, I thought I'd try.

My verdict: boxer briefs.

Walt:

Today I decided to do an experiment about flipping a coin. I was pretty sure heads would come up more since I like heads better than tails, and I also thought that heads was heavier than tails.
I decided to flip a quarter 100 times on my dining room table. The coin could not fall off the table; that

didn't count. My wife asked what the heck I was doing and I told her not to bother me, I'm conducting a very important experiment.

1st quarter: heads 10 tails 15
2nd quarter: heads 28 tails 22 – Way to go heads! Just like I figured!
3rd quarter: heads 38 tails 37 – Still winning heads, you can do it!

4th quarter:	heads	tails
	39	39
	40	40
	42	42
	45	45 – This is going down to the wire 10 flips left!
	45	49 – Heads is in serious trouble.
Final:	47	53

Moral of the experiment: Always pick tails. I don't think this was a good experiment for me. I got too nervous at the end pulling for heads.

Challenge #6:

Daydream Believer

No dream is too big or too small for a child. Fairy tales are filled with fanciful stories of impossible dreams coming true. Our niece recently told us that when she grew up, she was going to be an artist, a cheerleader, and... a bunny. As we go through "the system," getting indoctrinated with "how the world really works" and being taught to be "realistic," this imaginative anything-is-possible attitude fades away. But should it? We should all be thankful that Thomas Edison, Orville and Wilbur Wright, Rosa Parks, Henry Ford, Mahatma Ghandi, Neil Armstrong, and Oprah Winfrey (just to name a few) were not limited by what the conventional wisdom of their time deemed "possible."

The Challenge: Write down one big dream of yours. Draw or find a picture to go with it and put it somewhere you will see it often.

Kim:

Why am I going to put a picture of a license plate on my fridge? Well, one of my big dreams is to visit all 50 states. I think it would be neat to collect license plates from each of the states I visit. Jason and I hope to have a fun and playful basement family room someday. I would like to display the license plates throughout that room. So, I've found a picture of a license plate to remind me of this big dream. At this point in my 27 years, I've visited 17 states. Just 33 to go!

Jason:

When I was a little kid and my family would go on road trips, my brothers and I would eagerly peer out the windows. The object of our gaze: cars. More specifically, cars we would claim as our own. Any time one of us would see a car that we'd love to have someday, that person would yell, "Mine!" Once you claimed it, the car was yours.

I especially loved driving near Chicago. Having grown up in a small town, the selection of really cool cars was, shall we say, limited. The closer to Chicago you got, the better chance you had of seeing a Ferarri, Corvette, or my favorite, a jet black Porsche. It was really important to be alert; you surely didn't want your sibling stealing away the car of your dreams.

Ever since childhood I have always wanted a Porsche of my own. A real one.

Today, while walking to dinner with Kim in San Mateo, California, we spotted not one Porsche, but two. She reminded me that she had brought along the camera. I snapped photos of each, and plan on displaying them when we return home. I'm not sure what model I'll get when that day comes, but I know what color it will be.

Alex:

My dream is to be a professional drummer, playing venues all over the world and living the, well, not the rock 'n' roll lifestyle exactly, but a good life in which I play music for a living, and it doesn't feel like a job. On my monitor is a little drumkit alarm clock. It's actually a bit rough these days, and mostly in bits, but I keep it there anyway to remind me of when my journey began.

Jenna:

One of my big dreams is to have a room with at least one wall that is floor-to-ceiling bookcases. I recently went to IKEA® and saw several great displays and combinations. I have the brochures I picked up and I've got some photos from online. I made a little 3D display and put it in my bedroom.

Walt:

Anyone who knows me knows that one of my biggest dreams is to write a book. I have the title, intro and some life lessons done. No surprise, I also have the illustrator lined up (my son).

I drew a picture of me approaching a desk with a pile of my new books on the desk. Rushing to get an autographed copy are my screaming fans. I will post this artistic treasure on my writing desk.

Special note: The art talent skipped over me. That being said, I was still impressed by my artwork, but I am easily impressed!

Indulge Thyself

One reality of adulthood is that we have way more responsibilities than a child does. There's not much we can do about that. When we're kids, we dream of the day when we'll be able to have all of the power that comes with being grown-up. Well, with great power comes great responsibility, as they say. We all have people who depend on us, and it can be pretty easy – and admirable – to find ourselves putting their needs above our own. But the reality is that if we don't take a little time for ourselves now and then, we won't be any good to anyone. Which is not a good thing.

The Challenge: Spend 15 to 30 minutes doing something you love that you don't often have the chance to do.

Kim:

Today was one of those days that was jam-packed from start to finish. Everything was on a schedule. There was not much wiggle room for doing things I love to do. However, Jason and I did have about 45 minutes to kill before our speaking event this evening, so we went walking in this quaint downtown area of our destination and spent about 25 minutes in a local mom-and-pop bookstore.

Instead of going to the business books or even self-help books (which often feels like work), I picked up a book on fashion. I enjoyed sitting there reading about different clothes that my "body type" should and should not wear. I love just sitting in bookstores and picking up fun books. Too often I read for work, not fun. Why? Because it's more productive. This challenge helped me to realize that I don't always have to be doing something productive.

Jason:

I am an artist, and I love what I do. But it's been a while since I've drawn just for fun. I used to do it all the time, of course. Recently, I looked back at some of my old artwork. I used to do more portrait work and montages. I look back fondly at my time in school when I spent a lot of time experimenting

with different media and subject matter. I've been looking forward to a day when I would get back into doing art for art's sake, almost like a hobby.

So today, even though I'm in San Francisco, miles away from my trusty art supplies, all I needed was a pencil and a complimentary Wingate Inn paper pad to sketch Boba Fett. It was fun, relaxing, and stress relieving. Imagine that.

Jenna:
Tonight I indulged myself by spending time doing "Search-a-Word" puzzles. My grandfather used to do them all the time. I can remember as a little girl sitting on his lap "helping" find words – even when I just knew my letters. I learned several tricks from Grandpa Regis and they all came back as I was searching tonight. Such fun and a great memory!

Marisa:
Yesterday, I really wanted to go play on the swings at the park near my house, but the frigid weather kept me from that. So I thought of something indoors that I haven't done since I was like, 25 — spinning. I spun around in circles in my living room with my arms spread wide and then I'd lie on the ground and enjoy the spins. Only problem: 15 minutes is a really long time to spin!

Doug and Katie:
Tonight, instead of popping in a movie or spending the night watching TV, we got some reading material and just enjoyed each other's company without any distractions. It was a nice night.

Challenge #8:

##

Pretty much every kid loves to draw, whether they are any good at it or not. Once we start comparing ourselves to others, the majority of us stop, leaving anything artistic to the "creative types." Spending a few minutes doodling is a great way to tap into that lost childlike spirit. Have fun with it; who cares if it won't be hanging in the Louvre? This challenge also incorporates the element of surprise, which serves as a sort of fun and silly cherry on top.

The Challenge: Draw a funny picture and hide it in an unexpected place for someone else to find.

Kim:

I spent almost all of today on planes heading home from California, so this gave me some prime opportunities to hide a funny picture. If you've ever flown, then you are undoubtedly familiar with the *Sky Mall* magazine that is located by the puke bag in the seat ahead of you. I thought this would be a perfect spot to tuck away a funny hello. I specifically decided not to include it in the airline safety information booklet because no one ever really looks at those. It would be years before someone found my picture there. I wish I could hide a miniature video camera to catch the reaction of the person when they find this picture. I even wrote on there to check out www.EscapePlanBlog.com to see why I did this. Who knows, maybe that person will comment on today's post about finding it.

Jason:

I had to take advantage of being on a plane today. I pulled out the "motion discomfort" bag (which I am both happy to say I've never had to use and sorry to say I've never been able to see anyone use) to serve as my canvas.

I thought of putting some uplifting or encouraging words for the person who may ultimately use it. A little Hallmark® moment, if you will. For some reason, the thought of Garth from *Wayne's World* came to mind. Specifically the part when he said, "If you have to spew, spew in this."

That gave me inspiration for a great illustration — the bag needed a little gussying up. I'm sorry to say that the likeness of Garth was marginal at best. It's not like I had an arsenal of reference photos at my disposal (and if I did, I would've gladly traded them for more leg room). My imagination runs wild thinking about the people who will end up seeing my little work of art, hoping they'll giggle hysterically and pass the bag around the whole plane for a big laugh. Party on!

Or maybe they'll look at it and say, "Who's this supposed to be?"

- -

Alex:

One of my favourite sayings is "In the words of Gromit…", the irony of which is that Gromit (of the famous *Wallace & Gromit* cartoon duo) never actually says a word. So, in a quiet moment today at work, I doodled a little picture of Gromit, wide-eyed, with the words "In the words of Gromit…" underneath and left it in one of the magazine racks. I can't say the likeness was overwhelmingly exact, but I think it looked a bit like him.

Jenna:

I got to break out the markers, crayons, and even glitter glue for my drawing. My friend Sue just left on a trip to New Mexico and I hid my drawing in her suitcase! Hopefully when she finds it, she'll smile! It's got to be better than those "we've examined your suitcase" flyers.

Jaimie:

Tomorrow is "playgroup" and I'm going to hide a picture in the hostess' house. I'm thinking maybe in the microwave. Hmmm, don't want to burn her house down though…
[Update: I just wanted to let you know, I decided on putting the drawing in her freezer. I made a very silly face with a speech bubble that said, "Brrrrrrrrrrrrrrrrrr!! It's cold in here!" Hope she smiles when she has to get the frozen corn.]

Ian:

As soon as I heard this task, I knew exactly where I wanted to put this picture. What I didn't know was what to draw. Anyway, it struck me while I was listening to the Ricky Gervais Podcast: I would draw a warning sign. The next person to sit down in the first toilet cubicle at work will have that masterpiece to stare at while they do their "busy-work."

Rebel With A Cause

A little boy notices that his mother is having a rough day. The tone of her voice seemed upset during that last phone call. She smiles at him, but she looks sad. The boy rushes outside, and about ten minutes later, he returns triumphantly with a fistful of limp dandelions and wilted violets. Mom's day just got a little brighter. Children have a natural compassion that is sincere and selfless. Their compassion and desire to help is truly divine.

The Challenge: Do one thing today to support a cause or issue you really care about.

Kim:

Jason and I have been working with Compassion® International sponsoring a little (not so little anymore) boy from Ethiopia for the past 9 years or so. I try to write to him a few times a year, but often feel guilty that I don't more frequently. I've heard that you can E-mail your sponsored child, but have yet to take the time to  set up an account on their website. So today I set up my account so that I can keep in touch more easily with Hal. I sent him a Happy Birthday message right away, since his 14th birthday is at the end of the month.

I also wanted to show support for Compassion in a way other than writing a check, which seems like the easy way out for this challenge. So I found their "contact us" form online and sent them a message encouraging them in their ministry. I would guess that it would be easy for people who work for charitable non-profit organizations to lose sight of the differences they are making in others' lives. So I shared with them how much Compassion has affected my own life, as well as Hal's. Compassion embodies one of my favorite verses from the Bible, "And whoever welcomes a little child like this in my name welcomes me." (Matthew 18:5)

Jason:

After dismissing any thoughts of writing a million dollar check to The Make-A-Wish® Foundation, I thought about how often children draw pictures to show their support. I was inspired to use my artistic skills to lend a hand to a cause I have been supporting. A while back in my blog, I mentioned a small — but growing daily — group called Adam's Ants who have banded together to support a town in Mississippi that was ravaged by hurricane Katrina.

A recent e-newsletter mentioned that they were looking for some sort of logo to use in their newsletters, flyers, and web site. Now this was something I could do. It's been in the back of my mind, but today's challenge inspired me to make the time and just DO it. I'm hoping it will be well received. To me, it served as a needed reminder that we all have special gifts that can be used to make a difference — even a small one.

Alex:

For a while now, I've wanted to donate in some way to Great Ormond Street Hospital in London because they do the most important work in the city, namely looking after sick kids. Well, today I went one better than a donation and joined Friends of GOSH, which is part of GOSHCC (the hospital's Children's Charity) and helps to raise money for essential things the hospital needs. My mum used to work for the hospital, and I'm really glad I've finally done this.

Marci:

I think shopping online is a wonderful thing – I buy everything from stamps to all of my Christmas gifts online. And I'm able to support a worthwhile cause at the same time! I'm a member of igive.com, a site that has hundreds of name brand online stores and websites that will donate a percentage of your purchase to the charity or not-for-profit group of your choice. I'm choosing to donate to Twinless Twins Support Group, a group that I'm a part of, that supports individuals who have lost a twin. It allows me to donate throughout the year in a pretty simple way. Who knew buying my computer paper would be so philanthropic?

And about a Kim & Jason® related cause, I've coordinated my own "escape plan" of sorts – Operation: Escape Adulthood. Since I read Jason's book, I decided that I know MANY "stressed-out grown-ups" that could benefit from his eight secrets. So I've ordered several copies of the book, and have been sharing Jason's wisdom with people around me (free of charge, which is a totally cool surprise to the recipients!).

Today I shared four books. Three went to co-workers of mine, and one to a patient of mine. It was so great to see their smiles and excitement to read the book! So far, I've passed along 26 copies of Jason's book to my friends, family, my mailman, and our hospital's CEO!

Sue:

When I think about a cause I care about, many come to mind, but one that has had a personal impact on my life is Camp Courageous of Iowa (www.campcourageous.org). I volunteered with the camp for several years when I was a teenager. It's a camp for people of all disabilities of a wide range of ages. The things I learned and the friendships I made are indescribable and still hold a very fond place in my heart. Today, I finally wrote Charlie Becker, the director, to thank him and all the people (staff, volunteers and campers) for touching my life and to let them know how much their service makes a difference. Even though I haven't worked at the camp for 11 years, I still call it home in many ways. I hope that someday I will be able to give back again to them for all they have given to me.

Memory Maker

Think about your most treasured childhood memories. We'd be willing to bet that the ones that stick out have nothing to do with "things." Rather, the memories that we cherish the most involve unforgettable shared experiences with people we love. When life gets busy and we want to acknowledge somebody in our life, it can be easier to spend money on things rather than give up our time. With this challenge, we encourage you to create something that will last.

The Challenge: Create a memory today with someone you care about that will mean a lot ten years from now.

Kim:

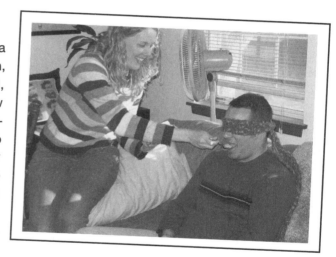

When Jason and I were dating, I made it a habit to bake him cherry pies every so often, since that is his all-time favorite dessert. Well, I have slacked and he reminds me every now and again of this. Now that we've been married almost six years, I am embarrassed to say that I can count on both hands how many cherry pies I've made him in our marriage. So I wanted to make this pie memorable. My first challenge was to make it without him knowing. Anyone who has been to our place knows that it is not that big. How was I going to bake this without him seeing me and also smelling the yumminess?

While Jason was in the shower this morning I hurried up and put the pie together and somehow managed to hide it in our fridge behind a big bag of romaine lettuce. Now, to hide the smell of it baking. Well, thanks to a *Kim & Jason* Sugar Cookie candle which I lit, the whole place smelled like cookies. It managed to hide the baking smells of the pie. I snuck in the kitchen after lunch and put the pie in the oven and snuck it into our bedroom to cool. When it was time for an afternoon snack, I called Jason to sit on the couch with a blindfold. He was pretty nervous, not having a clue what I was about to feed him. "Is it cherry pie?!" It was quite a surprise! How is this going to be memorable ten years from now? I plan on it being the last pie I make for ten more years.

Jason:

To me, nothing says memorable like a good kidnapping. At noon today, I hijacked Kim and Jenna from their regularly scheduled day. After blindfolding them with scarves and making sure they couldn't see anything, I guided them into the car.

Feeling the need to try and throw them off the scent, I took the roundabout way to McDonald's®. I took their Happy Meal® order — I'm addicted, see Challenge #3 — and proceeded through the drive-thru. Surprisingly, no one at McDonald's seemed to notice that I had two blindfolded women in my car. Apparently, that sort of thing is commonplace.

I did get a few strange looks from passersby on the way to our final destination: the zoo. At that point, I allowed the hostages to remove their blindfolds. It was a very

unseasonable 49° day and would have been a crime to not take advantage of the sunshine. We settled in for a nice lunch with the lions (our bench was across from the lion cub exhibit). They came up pretty close; I think they were attracted by the aroma of fresh hot cheeseburgers. Afterwards, we went for a nice stroll through the zoo. The only downside was the lame-o Barbie® necklace we got in the Happy Meals.

Ian:

My wife and I wrote love letters to each other and then sealed them up and put them in a frame, which is now hanging above our bed. Ready to be opened in 10 years time.

LuAnn:

Make a Memory!!! My daughter Heather and I got away to Mineral Point, Wisconsin and had a riot. We enjoyed the scenic trip with the rolling country hills and white blankets over the fields. We visited Styles Unlimited to get our hair done and then went to a luncheon. From there, we continued with shopping and viewing the arts of the town, then checked out the Bargain Nook, and, last but not least, visited Frank's Warehouse for treasures. It was wonderful just spending time together and are looking forward to the next time we visit Mineral Point.

Jaimie:

Today is my good friend Jenna's birthday. I decided to try and make this a memorable one for her. On the way to her office, I stopped and got a box of Krispy Kreme® donuts. Before hoisting her out of the car, I got my daughter dressed up in her best party attire (leopard ears and a lilac skirt complete with sparkles and white fur trim). Final piece of preparation: sitting on the top stair, I lit 12 candles in the donuts, trying not to burn down the place or light my daughter on fire. As we walked in singing "Happy Birthday," Jenna had a good surprised look on her face. Ah, maybe she was just noticing that the box was on fire. Happy birthday, Jenna!

You're Not The Boss of Me

The thing about grown-ups is that they always get the final vote. They have full veto power, and they're not afraid to use it, no matter how convincing a four-year-old's argument may be. One of the great fantasies of childhood is to someday be out on your own, free to call your own shots and do whatever your heart desires. Of course, it doesn't take a long stretch of early adulthood to figure out that being on your own isn't quite as carefree and fanciful as imagined. Although the call to be sensible and responsible is loud and clear, surely there is something you've always wanted to do that got vetoed when you were a kid. Now's your chance.

The Challenge: Do something your parents would never let you do as a child.

Kim:

The word "never" in this challenge really stumped me. My parents were strict but not militant. As I thought about it, most of the things they never allowed us to do were really for our own safety. After some soul searching, I realized there was one thing: eating dessert first. My parents would never have allowed this. Now that I am in charge, why don't I do it more? Jason and I decided to head out to dinner, so I picked Olive Garden® because I remembered seeing a yummy dessert that I'd like to try – chocolate lasagna. When it came time to order, I told the waitress I would be ordering dessert first. She admitted that she would like to do that more but feels too embarrassed. It did feel "wrong." I ended up getting an appetizer for my entrée. I was so stuffed. I felt like quite the dinner rebel. I highly recommend it!

Jason:

When I was a wee lad, I was enamored with Play-Doh®. Especially the smell and the way it felt in my hands. I even had a Play-Doh play set: the Fuzzy Bumper Barber Shop. It was awesome. There was a little plastic guy with holes in his head. You'd jam Play-Doh into his noggin and put him on the barber chair. As you'd push down, the compound would squeeze out of his head, creating a beautiful head of pink or blue or brown hair. There may have even been a beard/shaving element to it as well.

The trouble was that my mom never let me play with it. Ok, maybe that's a slight exaggeration, but I swear I can count on my hand (with a few fingers chopped off) how many times I did. On the blue moon when I was allowed to play with it, it was at the kitchen table. I remember being surrounded by some sort of plastic tarp, and a hermetically sealed white NASA space suit might have been involved. Any time I asked for one of those Play-Doh food kits — I LOVED those tiny hamburgers — I was always denied.

Today I went out and bought myself the Fuzzy Pet Parlor for $7.49. It was the closest thing to a barber shop I could find. I got home and created some very trendy hairstyles on various pets. I even — get this, Mom — played with it on the carpet! How liberating.

- -

Doug:

I did a couple of things that my parents would strongly disagree with. I stayed out past my curfew. I stayed awake until 2:30 a.m., and I ate ice cream for breakfast. So eat it, parents.

Alex:

My mum is a pretty liberal person and didn't disapprove too much of whatever I did back in the day, apart from one thing: banging on things. It. Would. Drive. Her. Nuts.

Like many kids who want to be drummers (uh-oh!), I'd take whatever looked like drumsticks and bang on anything resembling a drum: pots, pans, tubs, jars – whatever came to hand. Well yesterday, I decided to make a drum kit out of everyday items, and play along to one whole song.

My bass drum was a small washing basket laid upside-down on the floor; my snare was a casserole pot; my tom was a frying pan; and my ride was a Chinese wok (all placed on the coffee table). A pair of knitting needles were my drumsticks. Needless to say, the racket was LOUD, but AWESOME! I played along to *The Riverboat Song* by Ocean Colour Scene and had a blast!

Jenna:

This morning I did something I've always wanted to do growing up – I slid down the bannister! I think my size may have taken a bit of fun out of it as it is not a super long bannister therefore making for a short ride. Even though I'm 33-years-old, I still felt a little thrill in "sneaking" a ride!

Challenge #12:

We all had heroes growing up. Be it a masked avenger fighting the bad guys, a world champion sports star, or a favorite teacher, heroes give us something to aspire to, a glimpse of what could be. They provide hope, inspiration, and sometimes shelter from the storms of life. Taking time as an adult to reflect on your childhood hero is a great opportunity to rekindle those memories and values that helped shape you into the person you are today.

The Challenge: Write a letter to a childhood hero (real or fictional).

Kim:

My childhood hero was Mr. Fred Rogers. The half hour I spent with him each morning was one of the favorite parts of my day. His gentle, friendly nature taught me a lot about what it means to be a good friend. His adventures to factories and behind the scenes tours gave me permission to be curious about things I knew nothing about. After going to school for Early Childhood Education, I really appreciate Mr. Rogers' skills even more. His sincere devotion to helping kids and the methods he used to do that were genius! Since Mr. Rogers passed away almost three years ago, I decided to send my letter to his wife, Joanne. I am blessed that he was my neighbor.

Dear Mrs. Rogers,

I was recently asked to write a letter to my childhood hero. I immediately thought of your husband, Fred. As a child, Fred taught me so many things about life and learning. He encouraged curiosity and playfulness. His gentle and thoughtful nature modeled sincerity in friendships and integrity. Of course as a child, I didn't realize that the 1/2 hour a day that I spent with Mr. Rogers was teaching me so much. I just knew that he was my neighbor and I liked spending that 1/2 hour with him.

After receiving a degree in Early Childhood Education and teaching Kindergarten for 5 years, I had the chance to watch an episode of his show as an adult. I was blown away by the amount of learning that is jam-packed into that 1/2 hour in such creative ways. I saw his show through a whole new lens. Hearing his gentle voice speaking to me through the television reminded me how much he really affected me as a small child.

My husband and I work together now to help improve the lives of children and to encourage grown-ups to "Escape Adulthood" and return to childhood. It is not always an easy road, as I'm sure the road you and Fred journeyed together was also not that easy at times. I just want to thank you for supporting him and being his partner on the journey. My life has been forever changed by his ministry!

God bless!
Kim

Jason:

I wrote a letter to my boyhood hero, baseball player Ryne Sandberg. I am planning on sending the letter to him via the Cubs, with an old baseball card I'm hoping he'll sign. My brothers and I used to write to athletes for autographs when we were kids, so this was definitely a blast from the past. Here's the letter:

Dear Mr. Sandberg,

I wanted to take a few moments to thank you for all that you gave to me and the game of base-ball. I grew up a Cubs fan, and from day one, you were my favorite. I admired your blend of speed, power, and fielding prowess. Probably more than that, although it took me a while to realize it, I admired your integrity and professionalism. Because of you, I always wanted to play second base, and I got pretty good at it in high school.

As I've grown up, it appears that you're about the only sports hero I looked up to that still has his integrity in tact. That point was driven home pretty clearly when I heard your Hall of Fame induction speech. You stood up against the me-first attitude that has dominated pro sports and upheld the ideals of teamwork, commitment, and professionalism. It's too bad there aren't more role models like you.

I "retired" from baseball after high school to pursue my other love, art. But the standards you modeled while playing for the Cubs have stuck with me my whole life. I try to approach my career with the same quiet professionalism and dedication that you displayed on the field and in the media. I'd just like to offer you a belated congratulations on making it into the Hall of Fame, and thank you for being one of the good guys.

Sincerely,
Jason W. Kotecki

Jenna:

One of the things I loved most as a kid was reading. And while I read just about every kind of story, there were a couple of series that I was particularly fond of - Nancy Drew and Trixie Beldon Mysteries. So I sat down tonight and wrote a letter to each of the authors. While there have been many writers for the series through the years, both the original authors have since died. I think I might share the letters with the publishers of the series. As I was writing, I was remembering and I found myself totally back to that 8-, 10-, 13-year-old girl who lost herself in these adventures. I need to find those books again.

Walt:

In these times of people searching for heroes, it's too bad that people don't or can't look in their own homes. My hero is my Dad. And even though I haven't talked to him in over 37 years, I still think about him just about every day.

Dear Dad,

You may not have been aware of the impact you had on me, but it was huge and some of the things I observed and experienced years ago are still with me. I remember you coming home from work as a carpenter. You were worn out, but you still had a smile on your face. And I remember looking at your forearms. They were huge! Like tree trunks. I remember you taking me fishing and you finding the "hot" spots and then calling me over to try my luck as you went to find another spot. I remember all the volunteer work you did for the church and friends using your carpenter talents. I remember all the friends you had. Your pleasant smile made people feel good about themselves when they were around you.

I remember that "feel" that our home had: of honesty, integrity, always doing the right thing. And it always amazed me how your work ethic followed you years after you were gone. For many years, people tell me how my dad worked like two or three men, not one, and that he was the best carpenter they had ever known.

In closing, I would like to thank you for sending my father-in-law Harold around along with my boss Peter G. You put some good subs in!

See you around. Love, your son, Walter Marvin

Challenge #13:

Backyard Adventurer

Jason's childhood home had a small ravine next to it. Countless hours were spent exploring what seemed like a vast expanse of rugged terrain and lush vegetation. It could transform from an Amazon jungle to an unexplored alien forest over lunch. Kim and her three sisters made up all kinds of games that they played in their neighbor's pool. Spending time outside entertaining ourselves was a pretty regular occurrence. This challenge urges us to tap into that practice yet again.

The Challenge: Spend ten minutes doing something outside that you have never done before.

Kim:

Today I rode a skateboard. This is something I always wanted to do as a kid but never owned one or really knew anyone who had one that I could borrow. I was a little freaked out. It didn't help that I ended up trying it in the dark and on a slight hill. Yikes! At the beginning, I was a little overzealous and I decided to ride it down the slanted driveway. After almost losing my balance and wiping out, I decided that uphill was a good way to start – not downhill! It was fun, but I had a hard time enjoying it because I felt like at any given moment I would fall and break my head. Oh well, at least I can say I've done it now.

Jason:

Today's solution to this challenge put me into the "ridiculous weirdo" category. While laying in bed this morning, I tried to come up with something that I could do for today's challenge.

The big sticking point was the word "never." I'm no Boy Scout, but there isn't a whole lot of things I haven't done outside at one time or another. Okay, I've never jumped out of a plane, braved the rapids, or gone skiing, but these were not options today, for a variety of reasons.

One thing I love doing outside is walking. I do that a lot. And then I thought to myself, "Yes, but have you ever done it backwards?" Clearly this was a preposterous thought not worth pursuing, so I tried to come up with something a bit more "safe." And sane.

But it wouldn't go away. So at 8:45 this morning, I got out of bed, threw on my shoes and a coat, and headed outside for a 10-minute backwards walk. Part of the reason I felt compelled to do it was because I spend way too much time worrying about what other people think of me. Maybe not as much as some people, but more than I'd like to. Kids couldn't give a rat's rear end about what people think of them. I need to be more like that.

My backwards walk was a pretty liberating experience. Just a couple observations…It is very difficult to walk in a straight line while walking backwards. I'm pretty sure that people who saw me — yes, there were plenty of those — thought I was insane and drunk. Walking backwards takes a lot longer than walking forward, and I ended up using leg muscles that I didn't know I had. I got quite the workout, especially walking up hills.

Perhaps I have a new workout sensation on my hands.

- -

Doug and Katie:

Today we sang while standing outside on our balcony. It was quite fun! My song of choice was *Don't Cry For Me Argentina* - I couldn't resist really. Doug chose to sing *Me and Julio Down By The School Yard*.

Walt:

I love shooting free throws, so tonight at about 8:00 p.m., I decided to shoot free throws like I have never done before. I put on my PJ bottoms, slippers, heavy winter coat, stocking hat, and heavy leather mittens. I then headed out to the ball box in the garage to get a basketball. I have a favorite Michael Jordan black basketball that is so worn you can see the threads and the black is really gray. However, upon closer inspection of the ball box, I decided to use a full-size football instead and see how many free throws out of 50 I could make. As I was shooting, I was wondering if my final score would be a free throw percentage or quarterback rating. At first, it was fun as I worked on my technique (hold the ball with both mittened hands and at the point of push/shoot let the left hand pull away and shoot). However, then Adultitis showed its ugly head as I tried to see how good I could do at this and started getting ticked when I missed. I made 22 out of 50. I thought that was pretty good and I think with practice I could sink 30 out of 50. I did manage to swish a few, some clanged off the iron, and two rolled around the rim and out. Dribbling was tough.

Jaimie:

Like Jason, I had to think for a while about today's challenge because of the "never" stipulation. There are lots of things I've tried for about 30 seconds, but that's not never. So, after much thought, I decided to try bird watching. I have two speculations on why I didn't see too many birds today. 1) Time of year – lots of birds have flown someplace warmer, right? 2) The neighbor dogs barking just before sent birds flying away. I was amazed though at all the birds I could HEAR despite being able to see them. I guess my challenge for today was "bird listening with a little watching."

Ian:

I went for a walk around Darling Harbour yesterday. In the rain.

Neither of those are something that I have never done before, but…this time it was different. This time, rather than trying to get undercover, keep dry, stay warm, I decided to enjoy the feel of the rain. To relish it rather than resent it. I walked along the rapidly emptied harbour side, jumping in (shallow) puddles, feeling the rain on my face. My shirt got soaked through (there was nothing I could do to prevent that anyway), and I had the biggest grin in Sydney that lunchtime. I ran. I jumped. I laughed.

I got a few looks from the many people running to get undercover, hurrying their children along. People genuinely seemed frightened of the rain. I don't know why. It's only water.

I thought it was glorious.

Challenge #14:

Random Act

Children are so open to other people that they actually have to be taught to avoid strangers. This is definitely a good thing, but could we be losing something with this logic? Naturally, we spend most of our time with the people we know, trust, and care about. However, this can result in creating a "cocoon effect" as we tune out the other people around us. Humans were designed to interact with one another, and life is better when we do. One needs only to see the effect that touch has on at-risk newborn babies to see this truth in practice. It doesn't matter who holds the newborns – mom, nurse, or volunteer, just that they are receiving loving human touch. The world is made better when we break out of our cocoons and tap into our childlike inclination to reach out to strangers.

The Challenge: Do something to help someone you don't know.

Kim:

It seemed as though my opportunity found me today. I was walking into church when I saw a woman carrying a bunch of grocery bags from the church to her car. She was filling her car with the bags of food donated for the local food pantry. I asked her if she needed a hand. She welcomed my help. As I followed her inside to the church lobby, my eyes widened to see the "multiplication of the grocery bags." Holy donations, Batman! It was so nice to see how generous everyone had been. WOW. There were A LOT of bags. I grabbed a bunch and headed to her car. Seeing us going back and forth, another woman joined in. We had to stop eventually because church was starting, but the three of us picked up right where we left off after the service. As a team, we packed two cars fuller than full. It was such a great feeling to see a need and to help fill it. I sensed that the lady who had vol-

unteered to help was less than enthused about this job. Sometimes volunteers who get assigned a project end up doing it completely solo, which I've noticed can lead to volunteer burnout. It's a nice feeling to help a loyal volunteer!

Jason:

I didn't even realize I had completed this challenge until after it was over. (In fact, Kim had to convince me that it did, in fact, satisfy the conditions of today's challenge.) It all started in the dentist's office, my favorite place to be. Fortunately, I have the best dentist in the world (for those of you in Madison, Wisconsin, it's Dr. Brett Veerman of Dental Health Associates; tell him I sent ya), so it could definitely be worse.

One of my newest crowns — I have a growing collection — cracked last week, so I was in to have them take a look at it. As I was waiting in the chair, an unfamiliar hygienist came in with a fairly excited look on her face. "Are you Jason, the guy who does the artwork?" she asked. "Um, yes," I replied.

She went on to tell me that she had received one of my prints last Christmas, and that her daughter had seen me give a cartooning workshop a while back. She said that her daughter was a big fan of my comic strip, and had the print proudly displayed in her bedroom. "She's pretty modest about it," continued the hygienist, "but she's a pretty good little artist. And she really thought your presentation was cool."

I thanked her for the compliment, and offered to draw a little something for her daughter (I had nothing but time on my hands at that point). She found a piece of paper, I sketched little Jason and personalized it with some words of encouragement for her daughter. Kind of a fun little moment. I remember looking up to quite a few artists when I was in 8th grade, and a little note like this would have had me sailing. It didn't seem like much at the time, but maybe the note will encourage her to keep pursuing her passion.

- -

Doug and Katie:

Today we left a dollar on someone's car. We had a hard time coming up with something that would help someone else out. Neither one of us came across an opportunity during the day. After dinner, we snuck out into the parking lot and made someone a buck richer.

Jenna:

There is a daycare center up the street from where I live. They have a fenced in play area that borders the street. There always seems to be 4 to 7 playground balls on the street side of the fence. This is the furthest point from the entrance and I imagine someone has to walk out there every day to pick up those balls. So I stopped and chucked them over the fence tonight. Hopefully that will make someone's day a bit easier tomorrow!

Sue:

I decided to write an encouraging note to the person who owned the car I parked next to at work today. I don't know who owned the vehicle, but I wrote a note to Mr. Red Explorer telling him/her to have a great weekend; enjoy time with friends and family; laugh often and dance like no one is watching; may your life be blest and may you be a blessing to others. I hope this little note makes the driver smile and pass it along to someone else.

Challenge #15:

Taste Bud Conspiracy

"Try it, you might like it." We both remember sitting at the kitchen table when we were kids hearing more than once this suggestion from our mothers. Mothers really do know best. Normally, this statement was part of a plea to get us to sample the asparagus, but it also hints at a deeper wisdom and encourages a childlike spirit of adventure. Many of us, when we go out to eat, order the same things over and over again. By trying something different once in a while, we expand our horizons and go a long way toward thinking and acting in a more childlike way. Of course, for the purposes of our original foray into The Escape Plan, we gravitated toward the more extreme end of the spectrum. For this challenge, feel free to explore more palatable solutions.

The Challenge: Eat something you've never had before.

Kim:

When you're a kid, it's inevitable that you're trying new things all the time – sometimes after having to sit at the kitchen table for two stubbornly long hours. Well, as I walked around the entire grocery store, then walked some more, I realized that the things I haven't tried in my 27 years have been for very good reasons. I just couldn't get myself to pick up the little can of sardines (I almost puked just thinking about it). I am not that picky of an eater, so this was a challenge. Eventually I stood in the baby food aisle, deciding between beef and veal. I wanted to pick one of the meats, because, quite frankly, it is just nasty to think about meat in "baby food" texture. I have never had veal before, so I thought this would be a good way to go. The video of me eating this is  pretty graphic — total gag effect. It was far nastier than I even dreamed. It was so bland, yet smelled so strong. Meat should never be mushed. I almost spit it out. I know I would have if it weren't for that video camera in my face.

Jason:

Perhaps you remember the roasted soft squid from my visit to the oriental grocery store back in Challenge #1 (I know I'll never forget it!). I was very curious about that stuff, and originally wanted to buy a package, but alas, I had no cash on me. Well today was the day for my curiosity to be satisfied.

Kim picked up some squid for me while she was out running errands. I have to say, psychology got to me. Even though the food — and I'm using that term lightly — didn't look anything like squid, I couldn't get the slimy guy out of my head. I definitely know it's all psychological, too, because I NEVER think of cows when I'm downing a juicy hamburger.

It tasted sort of like shrimp or crab, which I like, but in jerky format. Pretty chewy. I can't say that it was terrible, but I certainly wouldn't go putting this in bowls for my party guests, which is what the display recommended. I once heard that in most cases, if you try something three times, you'll start to like it. Maybe I'll take another stab at it this evening and I'll end up becoming a squid jerky junkie.

- -

Walt:

Food. I have a love/hate affair with it I'll explain later. I was going to make this easy on me. First I thought of tea, then V-8, then tomato juice, and finally prune juice – the juice of regular seniors. But you drink that stuff, not eat it.

So tonight Linda and I returned to the scene of the Kiddie Cocktail restaurant, and I thought I would sample one of Linda's favorites: liver! I figured this would be easy because it would be deep fried and covered in batter. This would surely drown out the taste. But surprise, it was only available sautéed in butter with mushrooms. Ouch! I sampled a mouthful and I chewed it really, really good, and I have to honestly say that it had the taste and texture of s#!%, I think. Luckily, I had a glass of water at hand. Here is my best childhood memory of food. On Saturday nights, we either had spaghetti or chili. Chili night was bad because I hated my mom's chili. Odd as it seems, she would never drain the grease from the "thrifty" hamburger. The kidney beans would float on the grease like sailing ships on the Atlantic. The rule in our home was that if you didn't eat supper, you got it the next day for breakfast – cold. Now imagine the kidney beans stuck in the hardened grease like sailing ships at the North Pole!

Jenna:

Today I hit the produce aisle at the grocery store and hunted for an untasted fruit or vegetable. After perusing several different items, I chose the mango. I have never had a mango before and was even unsure as to how I was going to eat it. I did a little research on how to cut it – don't eat the skin – and began the process of cutting up the mango. It was a bit of a challenge, made more so by the flat wide pit. (I must have missed the diagram of the inside of a mango.) Anyway, it tastes and has the texture similar to a nectarine in the outer section and as you get closer to the pit, the texture changes to a more peach-like texture – softer and with those fiber-things. And overall there is a pine taste – in fact, I still taste that a bit now…I'm glad that I tried a new fruit!

Marci:

Tonight I ate vegetable potato pancakes – it was a mix. The vegetables were those small dried things, like I've seen in other mixes containing "vegetables." Red, green and orange specks were visible in the pancakes – meant to resemble onion, carrot, and the red? I'm not sure. Whether they were "real" veg-etables, I'll never know. The best way to describe the taste is like mixing potatoes with "Mrs. Grass" vegetable soup mix, or some other boxed dried vegetable creation. I'm sure the astronauts have it better. Not as high on the gag meter as Kim, but I'm definitely not making it again any time soon!

Challenge #16:

Family Tree Trivia

As we get older, we take a lot of things for granted. We think we know everything. This challenge is designed to open your eyes to some things you may have never considered before. It also tickles the curiosity bone and rewards you with a fresh sense of perspective on your own life. It's always interesting to explore the roots of your family tree and amazing to consider how events unfolded that ultimately led to the existence of...you.

The Challenge: Call or meet with someone in your family and ask them a question you are curious about regarding your family's history.

Kim:
My original plan was to call my oldest sister who lives in Texas. I soon found out that she has been blessed by a visit from the flu bug and was in bed. Plan B worked just fine, as my original questions involved my brother-in-law also. This gave me the chance to pick his brain a bit, which I don't often have the opportunity to do. He and my sister have been married for over ten years, and in their early days they lived on Ramen noodles in their small apartment as they tried to build Gene's business. Jason and I really look up to their accomplishments and appreciate the sacrifices they made early on to help get them where they are today. (There is no such thing as an overnight success.) I asked him to tell me about the biggest challenges they had in those early days and what helped them get through it all. He told me some things that I hadn't heard before. Knowing that Jason and I are still in our "early days," it was inspiring to hear what got them through it. I think sometimes pride gets in our way of asking others about their struggles and successes. We feel like we have to pretend we already have it all figured out. This challenge reminded me that there is so much I can learn from those around me. My brother-in-law's golden nugget advice was to stay focused and enjoy the little things!

Jason:
My Dad's letter from Challenge #12 inspired me on this one. (Yes, for those of you wondering, football-free-throw-shooting Walt is indeed my father.) He wrote about his dad – my grandfather – and it

occurred to me just how little I know about him. In fact, the first time I ever saw a picture of him was quite recently. His name was Walter, and he passed away when he was about 50; my dad was still pretty young. I got on the phone with my dad to see if I could dig up some more information about the one grandparent I never got a chance to know.

He grew up in LaSalle, Illinois on a farm, and spent some time as a factory worker and butcher before he settled in as a carpenter. According to my dad, family was the thing he cared about the most, and he loved spending time with friends and family. Apparently, he was a mighty fine euchre player and an excellent off-shore fisherman. My dad remembered him as a very social guy and recalled a funeral home employee saying, "Biggest wake I've ever seen for a lay person." That really impressed my dad, and he surmised that he must have been a pretty good guy.

That point was driven home when I called my Great Aunt Rose in a quest to find out just how my grandma and grandpa met. My dad figured that she might be the only person alive who knew the answer to that one. Unfortunately, she didn't either, but she couldn't say enough good things about my Grandpa Kotecki. "He thought the world of your grandma," Aunt Rose said. There was a lot of love between them. She did remark that Virginia wore the pants in the family.

"If it weren't for him, I wouldn't have such a nice kitchen," she continued. "We didn't have the means for it, but he remodeled the whole thing. He gave us free labor." She said that my grandpa was a good-hearted handy man, always doing favors for so many people. "He'd never charge them, either," she said. "He was so generous, he was always helping out somebody."

Looks like the mystery of how he and my grandma met will remain so, but as to why there was such a good turnout at his wake, that's pretty obvious.

UPDATE: I got a message from my Great Aunt Rose's daughter, filling me in on more details about my grandma and grandpa. Here goes:

"Apparently, your grandmother worked at a feed store and your grandfather used to deliver sacks of flour or grain (maybe 25 or 50 lbs each) or some type of supplies to that store. Mom said

that was how they met...My impressions? I don't remember having a lot of conversations with your grandfather, but I always thought he was a great guy who had the heartiest of laughs. Your grandmother was very proud of all of his handiwork and delighted in showing me all the cabinetry, closets or whatever he built. I thought your grandmother had the prettiest singing voice, and she played the piano and later the organ. She was a great seamstress and was no doubt the one who sewed the Santa costume that your grandfather wore when he came to our house on Christmas Eve. She once made herself a Little Red Riding Hood costume that she let me borrow one year. She used to do tatting (does anyone do that anymore?), and then there were her paintings. I always thought that your side of the family was blessed with so many artistic abilities."

Ian:

I asked my parents what countries I am from. Not literally from, but where our grandparents, etc. came from. We had dinner with my parents the other night, and I thought I'd take that opportunity to ask them which generations migrated to Australia. According to Mum, her dad's line runs back to the first fleet, but all her grandparents were Australian. Dad's grandparents were all Aussie too, except one (I think), who was from America.

If you keep going back, there is Irish, Scottish, German, English and a bunch of other European countries represented in there. I think we have some Scandinavian (or similar) in the blood too.

Sue:

For this challenge, I asked my mom and dad to tell me a story. My mom told me a story about when she and my dad were dating. They used to go to dances all the time – that's how they met (Ah, the good ol' days – when they actually had public dances!). One night, they were going to a dance, but there was an awful lot of snow on the ground and my dad went to pick up my mom who lived fairly far out in the country. My grandpa said to my dad as they were walking out (I don't think they had been dating too long at this point), "Grab the scoop shovel beside the barn, you might need it tonight." So, they left and it wasn't too bad near my mom's house, but as they got closer to the dance, the roads were pretty well covered. Dad ended up shoveling snow for quite a while so they could get to the dance. I thought that was kind of a funny story! I hadn't heard that one before.

Old Dog, New Tricks

Children have an amazing capacity for learning. The amount of skills and knowledge they attain in the first few years of life is astounding. Even learning a second language is easier for children than it is for most adults. But that doesn't mean we have to buy into the old adage, "You can't teach an old dog new tricks." Scientists believe that it is imperative to keep our brains active as we grow older, and adults who keep their minds sharp by trying new things are less likely to encounter dimentia or Alzheimer's. And at the rate of change going on in today's world, if you're not open to learning some new skills, be prepared to be left behind.

The Challenge: Learn how to do something new today. Your time limit: 30 minutes.

Kim:

It's been a long time since I really learned something new. My Adultitis has driven me to a place I call "Rutsville." Maybe you've heard of it? The days go by so quickly. The schedule is jam-packed. There is no slot on my To-Do list that invites or allows me to learn new things. So today I decided to learn how to tap dance. I think every child has pretended to tap with his/her "clicky" shoes on the kitchen floor. I thought it would be fun to learn a real move. Thirty minutes wasn't nearly enough. I don't own real tap shoes, so I stole a page out of my childhood and found some "clicky" shoes to use — my new red heels I'm wearing in my sister's upcoming wedding. They looked really good with my jeans. I'm so glad I didn't break a heel. I just love that sound!

Jason:

I remember putting on magic shows as a kid. You know, for my parents. I'd dress up in a bathrobe (not sure why, exactly), set up a TV tray to be my table, and boom, I was a regular David Copperfield. (I'm sure he started out in bathrobes, too.) I do not recall one actual trick that I did, but the fact that they were spectacular should go without saying.

I decided that 30 minutes was more than enough time to learn a magic trick (but not a very good one, as I found out 20 minutes into it). Not only could I perform it for the online video entry, but I could amaze my nieces, who are coming up for a visit this weekend. Well, it didn't take long to learn that the "super easy" coin tricks don't work too well when you have the finger coordination of a giraffe and the grace of a three-legged elephant.

Happily, I was able to perfect a dancing paper clip trick that delighted me to no end. With the help of George Washington (in the form of a one-dollar bill), I can effortlessly join two paper clips with the greatest of ease. At the risk of engaging in a bit of hyperbole, it will leave you absolutely breathless. Eat your heart out, David.

Jaimie:

When I was on the phone with my mom yesterday (see Challenge #16), she dropped her usual line "I wish just one of my girls would take up crocheting." For the longest time, I had ZERO interest. But I've been kicking it around and thought, "Why not?" I could maybe make a very fun scarf and have something to do instead of stuff my face in front of the TV. I would miss that though. So, while I know it won't take 30 minutes, I'm taking the plunge. I'm going to check out some how-to sites and even better, I'm going to e-mail my mom. Hey, she just may get over her fear of planes and hop over here with a needle and yarn!

Walt:

It's never too late to teach an old dog something new. Besides selling lumber and everything else you could imagine you'd need for your home improvement project, we also sell coal (yes, coal, that black stuff), sand, and various types of gravel in bulk. I can drive every vehicle at Maze Lumber except the tractor. So I had the yard manager, Craig, give me a lesson. I learned how to start it, stop it – YES! – and turn it off. The one we have is a two-speed with eight different levers. I worked the levers that raise and lower the bucket and cause it to load and dump the stuff. With my new skills I could go forward, backward and turn the wheel.

I learned to appreciate the skill it takes to run the tractor. I understand now how it was possible for our yard guys (the new ones) to place the bucket through the back windshield of a pickup truck (twice in one day). The levers can be tricky.

That being said, I feel that in just 30 minutes I have the skills to actually load up a customer with something. But just to be safe, maybe I'll load up something on one of *our* trucks first instead of a customer's $25,000 pickup truck!

Jenna:

Today I learned how to carve soap. Yes, soap. I spent about 15 minutes online reading about tips and tricks. Then to my delight, I found that I actually had a bar of soap in the house. (Remember when soap was a bar and not a liquid?) I spent about 15 minutes on my initial carving. The first person I showed it to knew right away what it is, even though it wasn't even half finished. It's a fun thing to do and easy to clean – the soap just washes away!

Prison Break

This challenge ties in with the previous one, and it deals with routines. Routines are good. They give us a sense of normalcy and they help us get more done. But they can very easily turn into ruts. Big, fat, boring ruts that are clear symptoms of Adultitis. After too long, these ruts become like prison wardens. They start running our lives, instead of the other way around. Every once in a while, you need to break free from the daily routine. Exercise your freedom. It's a big world out there; take some time to explore it.

The Challenge: Get out of your element. Go somewhere you've never been before.

Kim:

Jason and I were pretty adventurous (and poor) when we moved to Madison almost six years ago now, so going for rides was a pretty cheap and fun thing to do. We soon got to know where we were going and since gas prices have spiked, our rides have been less frequent. My goal today was to go for a drive and to get lost. Really lost. It took me a handful of random turns to actually accomplish this, but eventually I wasn't sure where I was. It was pretty fun! I drove around for about 15 minutes looking closely at the uncharted territory, noticing the different stores, neighborhoods, and scenery. It was pretty neat. I felt like Lewis and Clark, except I was in my Grand Am with my favorite CD playing…but it was pretty close to the same feeling, I'm sure.

Jason:

I suppose the best way to prove to yourself that you're somewhere you've never been before is by getting yourself lost. That's what happened to me today. We live near the University of Wisconsin campus and I decided that I wanted to check out the Geology Museum. The big draw: dinosaurs. I remember

being giddy with excitement when I was in third grade and we went to the Field Museum in Chicago. The big draw then: dinosaurs. I guess not much has changed.

After consulting a map, I thought I had a pretty good idea of where the place was. It took me forever to find a parking spot. I didn't have a lot of time, which pretty much assured that I'd get lost. I did. It was like looking for the invisible man at night.

I was starting to give up hope — and my parking meter was starting to give up minutes — when a nice girl pointed me in the general direction of where she thought it was. I set off in the opposite direction, with one last chance to find the museum before I had to head back to the car. I found it, and had a grand total of 12 minutes to explore. Luckily it wasn't that big of a place, and like a sun-baked paleontologist (frostbitten, actually), I discovered what I set out to find: huge skeletons of a woolly mammoth and a duck-billed dinosaur. Pretty sweet.

I got back to my car just as the parking nazi was about to notice my meter had finished digesting my change. Double sweet.

Then I was off to write. Considering I normally go to Starbucks®, I decided to stick with today's theme and try a new place — Ancora® Coffee — where I am now typing this. And after a cold windy morning of walking, the hot chocolate I ordered was triple sweet.

- -

Ian:

I read this task after having gone for a short drive with Jen. I think we fulfilled the criteria without even trying. Mat was being looked after by his grandparents, so we decided to go for a drive. Jen wanted to go to the beach, as we haven't been for about six months and we probably won't get much of a chance to go too often for the next six months either. So we started driving. We were not too sure where we'd end up.

We ended up at Collaroy - one of Sydney's Northern beaches.

We've both been there before (mainly with youth group camps), so that didn't count. But where we had lunch does: The Atlas, a restaurant in Newcastle. I haven't been to Newcastle since I was about ten, when we went to see my cousin (I think?) get canonized at the cathedral there. The restaurant did pretty decent food, but I wasn't too hungry as I'd had some hot chips at Wiseman's Ferry beforehand.

So there you go, a nice little drive to eat somewhere I've never eaten before.

Jenna:

Today I went to a restaurant I'd never been to before – a place that sells pies. Not just pies for dessert but pies for the main course, too. The menu is full of a wide range of cool choices: quiches for breakfast, pasties (a Cornish version of the pot pie) for lunch, and full entree pies for dinner. Some of the interesting combinations were: macaroni and cheese on a Parmesan crust, turkey and stuffing on a pastry crust, hot ham and scalloped au gratin potatoes, and lots more. They make several different ones each day or you can order your own combination. I chose the pork and apple pie. It was mostly pork with apple flavored type of stuffing. This excursion reminded me of trying new restaurants with my grandma. I would go to stay with her and we would go to all sorts of places around town. We had mixed experiences in food, but we always had a great time together! I think I need to try to keep the tradition alive and seek out new restaurants.

Jaimie:

This afternoon, I ventured to some place I'd never been before…sort of. It was a certain section of Sears. Yes, I've been to Sears before, but not too many times. Today, I was in the sporting goods area with the intent to purchase – now there is a place I've NEVER been. I learned about total horsepower, belt dimensions, manual incline, and am now the proud owner of a treadmill. Next challenge: actually using it!

Future Forecast

In his famous book, *Think and Grow Rich*, Napoleon Hill said, "Whatever the mind can conceive and believe, it can achieve." Much has been written about the often overlooked power of the subconscious mind, and it still remains very much a mystery to modern day science. What is certain is that more times than not, we tend to get that which we spend the most time focusing on. If we are usually worried, anxious, or concerned about what things might go wrong or how we might fail, mini-disasters and failure will follow us wherever we go. On the other hand, if we are constantly thinking about positive results and imagining a brilliant and exciting future, these things will come to pass. Believe that your dreams are possible. As Henry Ford said, "Whether you think you can or can't, you're right."

The Challenge: Spend 10 minutes visioning yourself 10 years from now as having accomplished one of your biggest dreams. Be as detailed as possible; imagine in all five senses.

Kim:

One of my biggest dreams involves having a family, owning my dream home in the woods by a lake, and having our company growing and affecting many lives in a positive way. I spent my time visioning "moments" of this life. One moment was a late summer evening, and my family and I were out on our deck watching the beautiful colors of the sun setting. As we all lounged in our chairs, we could hear the crickets chirping and the soft waves from the water. I was sitting in a chair holding one of our kids,  both of us wrapped in a soft fleece blanket to stay warm from the soft breeze off of the lake. I was holding a warm mug of hot chocolate. I could smell the pine trees, my child's hair, the fresh air. As I sat there and took in the evening, I was thinking about how blessed I was. I thought about our business and all that God has allowed it to become. I thought about the fun and creative office space we had just down the road. I thought about how much I love having kids and how much fun Jason and I have with them. I thought about how grateful I was to have this moment with my family on such a beautiful night. I can't wait for that night!

Jason:

I used the 10 minutes to imagine my dream home studio, located in the upper level of our dream home. One of the walls is almost entirely lined with windows, providing a breathtaking view of a shimmering lake. It's a late spring day, warm but not hot; a fresh spring breeze slipping through the open windows. The floors are hardwood, which feel cool to my bare feet. I'm sipping on a lemonade, sitting at my large drafting table. A few *Kim & Jason* strips sit finished next to a half-eaten cinnamon raisin bagel. Music is playing softly; a mix of Tom Petty, Jars of Clay, and Toad the Wet Sprocket, which reminds me of my college days when I dreamed of making it as an artist. The latest Mac is nearby — my guilty pleasure. Most of the other walls are lined with bookshelves, dotted with framed pictures of me and some of the people I've met over the years. A Reuben award (for best cartoonist) sits proudly next to some handiworks from my children. I've always loved the way the inside of Jamba Juice® smells, and Kim and I make it a habit to keep fresh flowers in the house, which is why the studio emanates a citrusy floral aroma. There is a smooth oak table near the center of the room. It serves as a spot for impromptu meetings, but is currently overrun by crayons, finger paints, and artwork made by my five-year-olds (yep, we've got twins!).

Ahhh…after a long, busy week, that's not a bad way to spend 10 minutes.

Walt:

By this time, my book will have been in print for a number of years and I hope to be enjoying the fruits of my writing; my legacy to my heirs. I will be at our vacation home along a quiet stream full of fish.

My grandchildren will be around me asking questions only grandpas can answer. As I take in the fresh earthly smell that kids acquire when they are outside, I'll close my eyes as I listen to their laughter. And I'll smile. The smallest of the bunch will be on my lap ready for a nap. It rests its head on my chest as I inspect the traces of dirt under its nails and I marvel at its tiny beautifully formed fingers. As I close my eyes again a tear of happiness rolls down my cheek and I'm reminded of the song, *What a Wonderful World*!

Jaimie:

Since it's often difficult to picture 24 hours from now, 10 years really threw me for a loop. I thought first about "the kids" and realized they would be 11 years old and 9 1/2 years old – fifth grade and fourth grade. I am so proud to be their mother; they are kind, loving and lots of fun to be around. They are serious at times, but have a fabulous sense of humor. When I wasn't volunteering in their classrooms or trying to keep the house in some sort of order, I wrote a book to help out moms - how to enjoy motherhood AND maintain your sanity with THE best publisher out there, JBiRD iNK. The book was selling well and I was off to New York City for a book signing. We decided to make it a family trip. As we got dressed to the hilt for the signing, I could smell my perfume, my husband's cologne, and the kids' hair care products. I used my favorite pen for the signing. Afterward, we went for New York City pizza and Cokes. We saw the sights, including the Empire State Building and Rockefeller Center. I could hear the life of the city – car horns honking like crazy. We enjoyed every second of it.

Marci:

I dream that in 10 years, I will have found the man that I'm meant to spend the rest of my life with (with the Lord's help). I can see the colors in the church, the dresses, hear the music, feel the tears of joy. We will honeymoon on Prince Edward Island. I can feel the soft, warm sand under my feet as we walk along the beautiful beaches, hand in hand, with the soft smell of the water, and beautiful orange and red painting the sky with a sunset. We will live in a quaint "country style" house with a wrap-around porch, complete with a swing where we will sit together in the evenings (after our kids are in bed), and enjoy a peaceful moment in one another's arms. And we'll live happily ever after….

Instant Karma

Karma is a term from Eastern religions that embodies the Law of Cause and Effect. The New Testament also teaches that "man reaps what he sows." (Gal 6:7) Or as the title character in the TV show *My Name is Earl* simply puts it, "Do good and good things happen. If you do bad things, bad stuff happens." This challenge offers an opportunity to balance out the ol' Karma scale and eradicate something that has been bothering you for a long time. Who knows? You just might sleep like a baby tonight.

The Challenge: Right an old wrong.

Kim:

My "old wrong" has to do with a promise I made to Jason and myself years ago. When Jason and I were just married, we promised each other that we would stay "in shape" for ourselves and for each other. We were both in high school sports and tried to stay active afterward, but it was much easier to slack off and not exercise once we went through college and beyond. Life just happens, and unless regular exercise is scheduled in, it just doesn't happen. Two years ago, Jason and I found a program that really worked for us: *8 Minutes in the Morning* by Jorge Cruise. I have been faithfully doing my 8 minutes of exercises every morning, but I know I also need to push myself further. I tend to do the "easier" exercises and skip out on cardio. Today I spent a while on Jorge Cruise's website reading articles about health and fitness. I read that if you don't have time to do cardio 30-45 minutes 5 times a week then you should do 15 minutes of interval training.

So I have made a new morning schedule which gives me more time, allowing for my 8 minutes, plus 15 minutes of interval training. I feel great about this recommitment to my health. I know that I always feel better about myself and have more energy when I make exercise a priority.

Jason:

Earl makes it look so easy. But maybe that's because I don't have a well of convenience store heists and have never faked death to break up with a girl. When thinking of a past wrong to make right, I went back to childhood for some less than stellar life moments. When I went to The Field Museum (see Challenge #18), I stole an arrowhead from the gift shop. I'm not really sure how to fix that one, considering I'm not sure that I still have the arrowhead — perhaps Karma took it back. But then I thought about my brother Dan. We had some pretty heated rivalries back in the day. I am responsible for a scar on his forehead that occurred when I threw a Fisher Price® school bus at him. I also had a big hand in breaking his arm on a flagrant foul while playing basketball.

Dan and I have grown up and have a pretty good relationship these days, but it occurred to me that I never really did apologize for some of these terrible crimes. I called him up this afternoon to apologize for the school bus incident, the broken arm debacle, and for generally being a jerky older brother. He accepted my apology with an outbreak of laughter. Silly, I know, but I do feel a little better to get that off my chest.

Walt:

Tonight I apologized to Linda for being such a jerk when we were dating (when I apologized, she laughed pretty hard). We dated pretty steady for five years before we got hitched, but boy oh boy did I ever rock the boat. Just about every spring I got spring fever and I got this crazy notion that I could do better and that I wanted to play the field – test the waters, so to speak. Every time I came crawling back like a jerk after friends and big bro told me I had the ONE for me already. I can't imagine what was going through Linda's mind as I did my annual stupidity stunt! But as a large mallet hits a cartoon character in the cartoons, I finally saw stars and came to my senses. And here we are 35 years later still together with three sons, three great daughters-in-law and 2.9 grandchildren! Sorry, Linda!

Jenna:

I'm not sure it would be considered an active "wrong" that I did to someone, but more of a "wrong of omission," if you will. Last Christmas, as in 2004, one of my cousins asked me to print off a particular photo of my grandfather from the family book I made. Until today, I had not sent it to her. It is printed and awaiting her address. I really do feel good about following through on that even though it's late.

Sue:

The other day, I was running through my mind the wrongs I've done and where to start in righting one. It came to my mind of something I did when I was a senior in high school against my mom. I had asked my aunt to make my prom dress before speaking to my mom about it. I didn't even ask my mom if she would have wanted to do it. I thought I was helping by not putting one more thing on her plate at the time, but in reality, if I was her, I would have been really hurt. Needless to say, when I had dinner with my parents the other night, I apologized. It felt good to tell her aloud because I still feel bad about that one. I told my parents they should start making a list of all the stupid stuff I did to hurt them when I was a teenager. My dad said, "One has to start with their own list before they can start making lists for someone else." Good perspective!

Challenge #21:

Thanku Haiku

When was the last time you wrote a haiku? High school? Never? We promised that The Escape Plan would help you think and act in a more childlike way, and we couldn't think of a better way to wake up your brain. For those of you who are poetically challenged, don't panic; no rhyming is necessary. A haiku is a simple three line poem. The first line consists of five syllables, the second has seven syllables, and the third line has five. That's it. We've added a twist to help you keep in mind the important things in life.

The Challenge: Write a haiku about the things you are thankful for and put it somewhere to serve as a reminder.

Kim:

Writing a haiku was tricky because I really had to choose the words very carefully. I can honestly say that each of the words I picked were "gold" to me. Only having 17 syllables to work with was frustrating, but in the end I think it forced me to pick out the things in my life that I really am most thankful for. So without further ado, my haiku (since I didn't rhyme in the actual haiku, I thought it was a nice touch to rhyme here)…

> God's peace, grace, joy, truth
> Jason, family, friends, health
> Childlike faith, hope, love.

Jason:

I had so much fun with this, I wrote two haiku. I submit the first to the "delight in the little things" category:

> ipod for my songs
> rainy days for reading books
> and stuffed crust pizza

...and this one for the "let's be serious for a second" category:

> kim my lovely wife
> a smile that cheers me right up
> she likes noodles too

- -

Ian:

> Gorgeous redhead. Yes,
> Jennifer is the one that
> I really love best.

Jenna:

> the escape plan blog
> helping me to be more me
> laugh play love dream big

Doug and Katie:

> July Three Zero
> Some Thought Failure Was Certain
> We'll Always Stand Strong

Sue:

> Family, friends, faith
> Happiness, blessings to count
> Thankful for this day

Challenge #22:
This Little Light of Mine

When watching the evening news, it's easy to become overwhelmed by all the trouble in the world. We feel powerless to do anything about it – at least anything of great consequence – and throw our hands up in frustration. Children, on the other hand, have a great optimism. They are delighted to make any kind of difference, no matter how small. In fact, they have the wisdom to see that the contribution they make is actually quite significant, if only for the person who is fortunate to be at the receiving end of their kindness. Children know – and we'd be wise to remember – that the little things can be a big deal.

The Challenge: Do something to make the world a better place.

Kim:

I think the world is made better one person at a time. I thought about the people I know and someone very specific came to mind: a man who I think makes the world a better place each and every day. He is a youth minister in a nearby church, and Jason and I have had the privilege to see him "in action." He is such an awesome role model and the genuine friendships he has with his students are definitely impacting the lives of these young people for good. We spoke to his students and it is obvious that they are inspired by his dedication and leadership. He and his family make many sacrifices for him to work in that job. It is tough to live on a church salary as the breadwinner and raise a handful of kids, but he is committed to his students and his ministry.

I think people like him need to be thanked for their impact. Often, they don't hear enough how much their lives are affecting others. So I typed up a letter to him (without signing my name) and told him how much he inspires me. I wrote some of the specific things I've observed him doing to help make the world a better place. I encouraged him to keep going, even through the hard times.

I wish I had the money to include a big check in the letter, so that he and his family could go on a weekend getaway to Wisconsin Dells or something. But I do have a coupon book that has some coupons for free things in the area, so I included a handful of coupons for free ice cream, gourmet coffee, cookies, etc. I hope the note brightens his day and inspires him to keep making the world a better place, one person at a time.

Jason:

I made a real effort to tackle this one with the mindset of a child. Maybe it's the retired superhero in me, but it seems to me that if you ask a kid to do something to make the world a better place, his first thought would be to think big. As in "whole world" big. This made me feel pretty insignificant; after all, what could I do to make the "whole world" better? Not even Oprah has THAT much reach. But I know someone who does, which is why I turned to prayer. I think God's got the most pull of anyone I know.

Ah, but what to pray for? My thoughts eventually turned to the Middle East. To be honest, I don't have a lot of hope for the Middle East in general. I think it's an Adultitis-enhanced form of cynicism that has developed in me over the years. I mean, that entire area has been a hotbed for violence since the beginning of time, what hope do we have for peace? But that's not how a child would look at it. To a child, ANYTHING is possible. He would send his prayer up to the big guy, fully expecting a positive response.

So I pulled out my rosary, recited the prayers I learned back as a kid in Catholic school, and tried to muster up as much optimism as possible for the Middle East. I prayed that good things would continue in Iraq, and that God would help that area blossom into a beacon of peace for the "whole world."

Idealistic? Naive? Perhaps. But very, very childlike.

Marci:
My new boss at work, Lauren, will start on Monday. I've decided to print up a few colorful "welcome" signs on my computer and put them up in her office. I'm also going to get a few balloons and maybe some flowers to brighten up her desk on her first day!

Jenna:
I think that improving the life of a child is a great way to make his/her world a better place. I also think that we have no idea how great of an impact that child will have on the future of our world! Today I made a special donation to the Medical Assistance Fund for Compassion International. I sponsor a little boy from Tanzania through Compassion and know through his letters how much having my financial and spiritual support means to his world. Sacrificing a few cups of coffee to help out with the medical needs of other children in Tanzania makes me feel like a kid who emptied her piggy bank into the Salvation Army donation bucket at Christmas time!

Sue:
Today I spent about 30 minutes talking to a colleague of mine whom I only see maybe once a month. She's normally a very positive, upbeat person, but she was going through a rough time and feeling really down. I just chatted with her and listened. I tried to really just listen. Even though I had planned a task list of things to get done, this was one moment I didn't hurry off or even think about my own things to do. It was a good feeling. I hope that I take the time to do that again sometime soon.

Challenge #23:

Photo Safari

This challenge offers up a little something for the adventurous side of you. Like Indiana Jones, your job is to track down something of great value, but what? That little mystery is up to you. It may be obvious, but it's more likely to be off the beaten path, hidden from the casual observer. One thing is certain, this challenge will be a true measure of how effective you're becoming in thinking and acting in a more childlike way.

The Challenge: Take a picture of the most childlike spot in town.

Kim:

I immediately thought of a shoe slide that is a part of the playground near Madison's Henry Vilas Zoo. I would've loved it as a child! It reminds me of something similar that I experienced when I was little. The McDonald's® that was in my hometown had a big Ronald McDonald car in the seating area, which actually had two built-in booths. I always hoped to sit in the "car" when we went there. I can only assume that kids would love to go to this park because of the "Old Lady's Shoe."

Just for fun I looked up the actual nursery rhyme to see how it goes and found the original version to be not unlike most original nursery rhymes: surprisingly harsh, which is probably why I found tons of "adapted" versions that were much more "PC."

Old version:
There was an old woman who lived in a shoe
She had so many children she didn't know what to do.

She gave them some broth without any bread,
Then whipped them all soundly
And put them to bed.

PC version:
There was an old woman who lived in a shoe
She had so many children she didn't know what to do
She gave them some broth along with some bread
Then hugged them all soundly and sent them to bed

Jason:

I would say that Ella's Deli is the most childlike spot in Madison, Wisconsin. But that doesn't mean it's easy to photograph. The place is an old-time delicatessen and ice cream parlor that features a classic carousel in the summertime. The inside is an overwhelming feast for the senses. The entire ceiling is populated by animatronic characters: a Superman that flies back and forth, keeping watch on diners below…tropical fish that spin 'round and 'round…a genie that skims through the air on a magic carpet. There must be a hundred of them — definitely over fifty — and I'd bet that Ella's is the electric company's favorite customer.

We took our nieces there last weekend for ice cream, and I was waiting for the youngest's head to explode due to sensory overload. (Speaking of ice cream, they also have a $38 sundae called the Sparkled Kazoo that boast 32 scoops of ice cream and sparklers for decorations.) I particularly enjoy the tables, many of which have detailed shadow box type displays — some with movable parts — which add a taste of nostalgia to the menu. Within the tables pictured here are old soda bottles and candy. Ella's website sums it up, saying, "The effect is one of entertainment for children and for adults who will remember many of the things from their childhood."

And that's why I think it's the most childlike spot in town: it offers up a serving of childhood to the young and old alike.

Jaimie:

Jason took my first choice – you can't go wrong with Ella's Deli. Yesterday, I was at a place that was a close second. Next Generation is a salon designed exclusively for children ages 0 to 14 years (that was the description on their website). I took my daughter for her first haircut and what a childlike place! She sat in a taxi cab (the other choices were a fire truck, duck and turtle), looked at stuff hanging from the ceiling, and watched a sock monkey on TV. Fun stuff.

Walt:

I grew up in a little town in Illinois called LaSalle. We had this one store in our neighborhood called Frank's Cigar Store. All the kids in the neighborhood would flock there regularly and spend every penny they had. The place smelled like cigars (no surprise) and Frank was a heavyset gentleman that never left his stool unless we interrupted him when we wanted to buy penny candy. I would stand in front of the glass case and get Red Hot Dollars, Smarties, Jaw Breakers, Pixie Stix, Milk Duds, Bazooka bubble gum, and wax bottles filled with juice, just to name a few. He had a full rack of comic books including Archie, Superman, the Fantastic Four, etc. He had soda jerks (and some of them were jerks) that made fountain Coke, Green Rivers, and hand-dipped ice cream cones. He also had the forbidden zone where the big boys hung out. Once in a while if you had to go to the bathroom really bad you could plead your case and they would let you go to the john past the secret area, sneak a peek of the forbidden zone, and report back to your buddies what you "saw." The place is still there, but it's not the same. Frank's was a childhood dream.

Marci:

There are TWO childlike spots in my town. One is the treehouse in the backyard of the house across the street from my parents'. It was built by the father of the family that lived there when I was growing up (about 20 years ago) and it is still there! Just looking at it brings back memories of my childhood and all the BIG adventures that come with a treehouse! And there is a park in the subdivision where my parents live called "Cinderella Park." There is an array of usual playground equipment, but the best part is a wooden replica of Cinderella's coach in the middle of the park. It's all for climbing around in and letting your imagination run free…

Outside The Lines

We remember fondly those giant boxes of Crayola® crayons, packed with 64 glorious colors – including such classics as gold, brick red, and periwinkle. When it came to crayons, you could never have enough colors. Whether it's a blue tongue from a Popsicle®, a red Kool-Aid® mustache, or a mismatched technicolor outfit, kids love color. And it's no surprise that grown-up life can get a little grey and monotonous. That all ends today!

The Challenge: Figure out a way to add some color to your day in a new, unusual, or wacky way.

Kim:

I am happy to report that we have had some very sunny days here in Madison recently. I had that in my favor today as I filled eight glasses (two wine glasses) with colorful water. I lined them up along my windowsill by my desk. I had a very colorful desk, with the sun shining through the many colors. I really enjoyed looking at the light and reflections throughout the day as the colors moved to different parts of my desk. Dropping the food coloring into the glasses brought back some great memories of dyeing Easter eggs, making Play-Doh® and most recently teaching our "Color" unit in kindergarten. (The kids would "experiment" with color mixing using eye droppers and colored water.) I really didn't want to put the glasses away.

Jason:

Dr. Seuss would be so proud. This morning, I took great joy in eating some GREEN eggs. Sadly, I did not have ham — or spray paint — but I expanded my breakfast rainbow by eating Capn' Crunch® in

BLUE milk and washing it all down with some RED orange juice.

I cannot even begin to explain the sensation of giddy joy that I felt when I saw my eggs turn green. With God as my witness, food coloring is the best toy EVER.

Jenna:

Today I went towards the edge of "wacky" in bringing more color into my life. I decided to wear my colors – all ROYGBV of them! Yellow long-sleeve shirt, red 3/4 sleeve jersey, orange short sleeve t-shirt, dark blue jeans and striped socks – purple, yellow, green, orange and red! Lots of fun and quite a few smiles throughout my day so far. And I've decided I need more fun colored socks!

Marci:

Today I changed the background on my e-mail screen to a cool shade of purple. My IM (Instant Messenger) icon is now an animated blue crayon drawing of a smiley face complete with "spikey" hair, and the IM background/wallpaper is more crayon fun: green grass, a light blue house, and a stick person family! My e-mail is now colorful and color-fun!

Doug & Katie:

We took this opportunity of color adding to wear two of the finest candy necklaces all day long. Katie wore hers as a traditional necklace, while Doug wore his like a hip biker chain hanging from his belt. We looked awesome and colorful. Hopefully we brightened someone's day.

Challenge #25:

#

One of the biggest symptoms of Adultitis is an overly comfortable comfort zone. Straying too far from your comfort zone can be a little scary. The chance of looking silly in front of a stranger, now that's just plain petrifying! Children, of course, are not afraid to look silly in front of anyone. They're having too much fun to worry about what other people think. We offer a warning: this one is a toughie. If you can successfully complete this challenge, consider yourself well on your way to annihilating Adultitis.

The Challenge: Talk in a phony voice or accent to a complete stranger.

Kim:

This was by far the hardest challenge for me yet. Why do I care what others think about me? I failed miserably the first time and had to "try again." My first attempt was at a will call booth at a concert we went to (Andrew Peterson's concert, which was awesome, by the way). I started with my British accent, which quickly turned into my Wisconsin accent (which means my normal voice). It was tough being face to face with this guy looking right at me. And my British accent really stinks. Bummer. That one stunk. So I had to try again. After the concert, we went through the drive-in at Wendy's® for some Frostys. This went pretty well. I followed through – from the ordering to visiting both windows. This challenge helped me to see how much I take myself too seriously. These people were complete strangers who I will probably never see again, yet my heart was racing. It was definitely an eye opener.

Jason:

Today's challenge scared the snot out of me. Talk about measuring how much you care what other people think of you! Of course, children don't think twice about how silly they might look to others; this is a "skill" we gradually attain as we grow up.

Kim and I drove down to Rockford, Illinois tonight for a concert. I found my perfect opportunity to take this challenge head-on at the McDonald's® drive-thru. My English accent was FAR from perfect, but I managed to place our order and thank two different window clerks as Kim tried desperately to muffle her boisterous laughter.

Perhaps I shall try to recreate my dialogue in the video* today, although I can only promise you'll not be impressed. The important thing is that I did it, ungraceful as it may have been, and dealt a mighty blow to Adultitis.

- -

Sue:
With a made-up deep voice and pursed lips, I asked a lady in the Museum of Science and Industry where the whispering room was. I had a hard time not laughing at the same time.

Doug & Katie:
Katie and I had a hard time keeping a straight face doing this challenge. I ordered a pizza with a deep James Earl Jones style voice, and Katie picked the pizza up with a darn fine Dolly Parton impression. Although people probably didn't notice it, we couldn't help but feel completely fake. We sounded so ridiculous, how could anyone take us seriously?

Jenna:
I approached the lady at an information desk and in a British accent (very popular today) and asked, "Excuse me luv, do you have a pen or pencil you could give us?" After she found a pencil for me, I said, "Thanks, duck!" I was chuckling as I turned away!

You can watch the videos Kim and Jason recorded for each challenge at www.TheEscapePlanBlog.com)

Mr. Smartypants

This is another challenge designed to stretch your brain. If you really want to be more childlike – and say adios to Adultitis – you need to keep your mind moving in new directions. If you're not busy growing, you're busy dying. This is a fun one, and will help you impress your friends with your vast intelligence. Coke bottle glasses with tape around the nose piece are not included.

The Challenge: Open to a random page in the dictionary and look at the first word on the upper left-hand side. Keep turning pages until you find a word you don't know. See how many times you can use this new word in a sentence today.

Kim:

My word was "dowdy." It has two definitions: shabby, not neat; and old-fashioned. I managed to squeeze in a few "not too dowdy" phrases, as if to say, "Not too shabby." I have to admit I didn't do a very good job in remembering. I usually tried to incorporate the word into my language shortly after Jason used his word (I'm trying to be honest here). However, at dinner I used it very appropriately when referring to something being old-fashioned. So I was able to use both definitions. I know that I am not one to use new words, so this was very different for me today and quite honestly, I had a hard time remembering to even do it.

Jason:

My word today was "entrechat." What??? Exactly.

> en·tre·chat n.
> A jump in ballet during which the dancer crosses the legs a number of times, alternately back and forth.

First of all, the word was extremely fun to say. It reminded me of the two years of French I had in high school (of which I recall almost zilch). It was so fun that I think Kim said it more times today than her own word. I was able to use it several times successfully in a sentence, including these highlights:

"I imagine that it would be quite dangerous to try an entrechat in the shower."
(Before taking a shower this morning.)

"I'm sure I'd capture their attention if I did an entrechat to open my talk."
(After Kim warned me before a speech I gave to seventh graders today that I shouldn't expect to get much of a reaction out of them, even if they are enjoying it.)

"I'd say the driving performance you pulled off tonight was more difficult than an entrechat."
(After Kim had successfully navigated congested Chicago traffic in the middle of a downpour.)

- -

Walt:
My new word was "sprent," which means "sprinkled."
I used sprent in these situations:
Last night I told Linda, "Your brown hair is sprent with gray."
This morning I told my boss Pete, "Your bald head is sprent with tiny grayish brown hairs."
Today I told one of my co-workers, "Your pants are sprent with tinkle." (I did say this but I made that up because I just wanted to.) He looked down and was quite embarrassed.
Finally I told Don at work when he was complaining about his problems, "Your day is sprent with problems."

Sue:

My word: disgorge. To discharge from the throat; to vomit; to give up (what one has wrongfully seized). Not a very pleasant word, but it worked quite humorously in a number of sentences. Just the mere fact of trying to use the word – even inappropriately – in sentences was probably the most hysterical part!

Jaimie:

The word I found was "afeard." (adj. Afraid.) This word was tricky for me to use, but I managed. I think I said something like "I'm afeard that we will have a hard time getting Belle to give up her pacifier." Even better though, was my use of the phony accent. We were at a very hoity-toity art show at this mansion in Kenosha and I decided to try out my Southern accent. Near one of the treat tables, I asked a group of ladies, "Do ya'll know where the bathroom is in this place?" (long emphasis on the "a" in place). The woman gave me a smile and directed me the right way. I'm not sure if she was smiling at the sweet Southerner or if she could tell I was faking it. I made sure to say "thank you" in my best Southern accent before the encounter was over.

Spin Cycle

Do you know how much of your daily routine is habit, performed subconsciously day after day? According to motivational speaker and co-author of the *Chicken Soup for the Soul*® series, Jack Canfield, ninety percent! Not too hard to see how easy it is to go through life in a well-worn rut when the overwhelming majority of your actions are the same. Life can get pretty boring, and as everyone knows, kids HATE boring. Here's your chance to do something about it.

The Challenge: Take a routine you do every day and put a childlike spin on it.

Kim:

Today as Jason and I walked to the car together, I put my arm around his shoulder and invited him to walk "like *The Monkees*" with me. Then on the way home from church, I stopped at the grocery store so that Jason and I could each pick out a doughnut. I always loved stopping for treats when I was a kid – whether it was ice cream from Dairy Queen®, gingerbread cookies from the bakery, or a Frosty® from Wendy's®. Little treats were always such a big deal as a child. Who am I kidding? They still are.

Jason:

Normally, when I think of a routine, I normally don't think of weekends, which is when this challenge fell for me. But it didn't take long for me to realize that I have some morning routines that happen each and every day, whether I'm working or not. I decided today would be "opposite" day.

I started in the shower. (Hey, get your mind out of the gutter!) I washed my hair first, which I normally do last. I put my pants on one leg at a time, but this time I put the right leg in first. Same thing with my socks; opposite foot first. I ate my breakfast cereal — Capn' Crunch® again — with my left hand. Then I brushed my teeth with my left hand, and this proved to be the most difficult task of all. I'm sure my dentist would not give me a high score on the thoroughness scale. At church, Kim and I sat on the opposite side that we normally do (I resisted the urge to drive on the opposite side of the street to get there). To top it all off, I ate dinner with my left hand.

And tonight, I intend on once more brushing my teeth with my left hand.

Marci:
I wrote my shopping list in crayon – purple, of course! (I haven't had Capn' Crunch® in ages, so I put it on the list!)

Walt:
This morning, I put on my usual white socks. But then I took them off and put on my Snoopy black Christmas socks. Then I made my breakfast. First, I poured milk into the bowl and added Hershey's® chocolate (stirring slowly until brown), dumped in Cheerios® and enjoyed. I was excited about getting done with the dumb cereal so I could drink the chocolate milk! I took a green mug from the kitchen cabinet for my coffee today. It was a Teenage Mutant Ninja Turtle City Sewer mug. I wasn't sure if it could hold hot coffee, but Pete said, "Don't worry about it, mom can clean it up!" Finally, I put away all my boring blue and black pens and used red, pink and purple today!

Doug and Katie:
The morning comes pretty early around here. We usually make it through without much talking or sound. This morning, we turned up the radio and it really did make our morning a little more fun. Some good oldies can cure anything.

Jaimie:
In the morning, I usually eat a "sensible," healthy cereal, and today I woke up with Cookie Crisp®. Then when I headed down for my time with the treadmill, I put my hair in pigtails. And I'm with Kim on treats, so maybe one will make its way to me today…

Ian:

I've started walking to work from Central Station, rather than catching another train for a single station. This walk takes about 10-15 minutes each way, so today I decided to walk swinging my arms in synch, rather than opping each other.

What am I talking about?

Next time you walk, you will notice that your arms naturally swing opposite to the direction you are placing the foot on that side. So, if you put your right foot forward, your left arm will swing forward to match it. This keeps your balance quite nicely.

If you make a conscious effort to swing your arms together instead of separately, you'll find your body moves differently while you walk, jerking back and forward at the end of the swing.

People also look at you funny. I don't know why.

Challenge #28:

Five Hundred Pennies

We loved when we went shopping with our parents and they'd let us splurge on something with our allowance money. It didn't happen often for either of us, so it was a real treat. Much deliberation took place as we evaluated our choices. Jason remembers peering over the concession stand counter after swimming lessons, carefully plotting how to get the most amount of candy for his money. Two Blow-Pops®, a packet of Fun Dip®, and four Laffy Taffys®. Even though you're all grown up with an income that's bigger – hopefully – than your allowance ever was, a lot of fun can still be had with a small amount of money.

The Challenge: Buy something that captures the spirit of childhood for under $5.00 (including tax).

Kim:

My "find" totaled $0.99. As you can see, it is a glow-in-the-dark eyeball bouncy ball. There is something magical about bouncy balls when you're a kid. Maybe it's their unruly and unpredictable nature, maybe it's because it's one of the only cool prizes in the gumball machines that you can afford as a kid. I'm not sure, but I think it definitely serves as a product that captures the spirit of childhood. Jason and I actually went into the dark bathroom to see how it glows. Boy, did that bring back memories.

Jason:

Two words: silly string.

Purchased at Walgreen's for $2.99.

I never really got a chance to play with this stuff when I was a kid (after the cleanup, I can see why). I had a blast ambushing Kim as soon as I got home. It was even kind of fun when she stole the canister and turned the table on me. I don't know who the heck invented this stuff, but something tells me they were virtually Adultitis-free.

- -

Walt:

The item that I always wanted to buy was a metal cap gun. Back then, there were lots of choices. The birthday present-quality versions were heavy metal with pearl-like handles that came with leather holsters and leather straps at the bottom to tie to your leg. Very pricey! Then there were the small everyday models that fit nicely in your hand. They were made of tin and usually rusted by the end of summer (sooner if you left it outside, of course it rained that night and then just before you went to bed, you remembered you left it by some rock). I came up empty on that find. I did go to Target® with the main purpose of getting a toy, and I thought about it all day at work. Luckily, I got off at 3:30 and Linda and I rushed up to Target. I calmly approached the toy department trying to hide my excitement. I looked at some card games and they were OK. But then Linda called me over and on one end cap there it was, the mother lode of old-time toys. They had about a dozen offerings, and I settled on not one, but two toys. You can do this when you are the boss (almost). One was a wooden catch ball (a wooden ball and nicely painted handle with a cup to "catch" the ball). Linda said I can open it after I eat my supper. I'm taking it to school – I mean work – tomorrow.

The other toy is a classic. I spent hours reading the back of cereal boxes wondering how and if this thing really works. It was unbelievable! Old boys, you remember this one, the diving submarine powered by baking soda. I don't take baths like I did as a tot, but I bet I could impress my granddaughters the next time they take a bubble bath!

Marci:

I bought three helium balloons today – they are a gift for someone else – but they gave me childlike glee as I carried them out of the store and into my house!

As for a $5 purchase for myself, I'd planned on getting ice cream tonight with a friend, but lo and behold, the ice cream place was closed when we got there! I settled on an apple cider at Starbucks®. It reminded me of the fall weekends we went apple picking when I was a kid! Fall is still my favorite...

I didn't get my "fun" ice cream tonight, but the apple cider was a good second choice!

Jaimie:

I also bought two items for under $5 today. I got FUN socks. One pair has different colored coats all over them. And the other pair really captures the spirit of childhood — light blue, cornflower, lavender, dark purple and white stripes plus a pink and blue butterfly right on my ankle bone. The cake topper: they came with a ponytail holder with a plastic butterfly on it. All for the bargain price of $1.

Sue:

I bought two items both totally under $5. With quite some giddiness, I bought a Frosty® from Wendy's® (99 cents). It's something I haven't had in a really, really long time, but I remember every once in a while as a kid, my mom would take me and my younger sister there. As soon as I took one bite, I was whisked away back to sitting there with my mom and my sister – and boy did it taste yummy. I also purchased a little toy replica of the Wright brothers' "Flyer" that made the first flight ever in a machine heavier than air in 1903. To think of the courage that it took Orville and Wilbur to dream up a contraption like that. It must have made lots of people think they were crazy! But they pursued their dreams, in my mind, with a childlike persistence to making an imagination become reality.

Challenge #29:

Just Like George

Curious George is famous for his limitless, um...curiosity. A healthy curiosity is a vital ingredient in remaining childlike. We all encounter a variety of interesting people every day, and we rarely take the opportunity to learn from them. All too often, we're afraid to ask a question because we're afraid we might hear, "What a stupid question! You must be the only person in the whole world who doesn't know the answer to that! Did you know that you're a complete idiot?" As silly as that sounds, how often do we pretend to know more than we do so we don't appear foolish? The reality is that if you ask a sincere question of someone, especially in an area in which they are well-versed, they will be flattered and think more highly of you because you took an interest in them. Try it.

The Challenge: Ask an expert something you are curious about in his/her field.

Kim:

A few years ago I met a very talented man named Jason Huett. He is a 3rd Degree Black Belt and founder of Kicks Unlimited. Jason's vision is to develop the greatest martial arts system in the United States – one where kids and adults of all ages could learn not only the martial arts, but also life skills in a positive and service-oriented environment. The thing I remembered right away about Jason is that he told me that he used to be a real Power Ranger®. I also found out today from his website that he has worked as a professional stuntman in Los Angeles for the movie *Legally Blonde* and the ever popular *ER*.

Needless to say, I had a few things I was curious about in his field. So I called him up and fumbled through the reintroduction of myself, after having only talked with him for two minutes two years ago. He was super nice and very open to answering my questions.

I asked him to explain for me his style of martial arts. He called it "extreme martial arts." He said that in the 80's with the *Karate Kid* movies, martial arts became more popular. His style combines some of his acting and stunt experience involving entertainment with acrobatics and martial arts. I asked him

137

about the choreography of the Power Rangers. Is it all choreographed perfectly and how long does it take to learn it? Jason shared that for the TV show, they would get on set that morning very early, choreograph the scenes for the day, and then shoot the scenes the same day. For the live performance shows he would do for Power Rangers, the moves were choreographed further ahead of time. They would try to "mix it up" here and there to keep adding harder moves and to add variety to their performances. Jason also shared that the talent in Hollywood pales in comparison to the talent in the karate schools across the country. The teachers in his classes are some of the most talented out there.

Of course by the end of our ten minute conversation, I was wanting to see some of this talent in action. Jason invited me to stop by anytime to watch any of the classes or even the tournaments. He also directed me to the NASKA (North American Sport Karate Association) website.

I have to say that this experience really got me out of my comfort zone and got my curiosity piqued in an area I know very little about. Jason's profession is fascinating, and it is neat to hear how much creativity and personal style he has put into his profession and business.

Jason:

In Challenge #17, I took the time to learn a magic trick (they're *illusions*, Michael). I only had 30 minutes and no chainsaw, so I wasn't able to figure out how to saw Kim in half (safely, that is). Today I turned

my attention back to magic. I happen to know a magician, and I figured that this was a pretty good time to ask a burning question:

Where do magicians get the ideas for their tricks? Are there special books they can buy? Do they create their own original tricks? Do magicians get together at conferences to learn new tricks? Here's what Robert said:

"All of the methods you asked about, I do. There's no easy way to answer your question. Yes, you can buy tricks and illusions and probably make them work OK. Remember though, it's kind of like buying Photoshop.

You can probably make it do what you want. But there are countless nuances and techniques that transform it from a software program into real magic. I've been doing magic for 31 years and I'm still learning. Best secret…it's not about the tricks or fooling people. It's about connecting with people and having fun. The real secret is to make stars out of your audience members."

Interesting comments, I thought. (Thanks Robert!) Upon further review, I uncovered a magazine devoted to magic and quite a few websites that turned up magic conferences. I'll be meeting with Robert in a few weeks, and I have a few follow-up questions to ask him then. So far, I have not been able to dig up a book that will show me how to saw Kim in half. (Safely, of course.)

- -

Jaimie:
Over the weekend, my mother-in-law got high honors for her quilting at a gallery in Kenosha, Wisconsin. I decided to ask the expert a little bit about her craft. Her theme this year is trees or woods. She explained the process of dyeing and bleaching fabric (also called discharging) to get the colors she wants. She paints on bleach – the stuff you'd buy at any store – and then uses this "stop bleaching" stuff. It was really interesting.

Sue:
Today, I asked a co-worker of mine about kayaking. She co-operates a kayaking and canoeing outdoor business. I learned more about kayaking on the open ocean or sea kayaking vs. lake or river kayaking, as well as the difference between wet suits and dry suits. She told some great stories of challenges, and people overcoming some dangerous situations. It was fascinating! Maybe I'll learn how to kayak someday, but I think I'll probably stick to just the calm lakes.

Jenna:
What do I need expert advice on? Hmm, how about the shoulder pain I've been having for a while now? Utilizing my insurance website, I was referred to a specialty page for rotator cuff injuries. I learned a bunch of interesting things about my symptoms and possible treatments and such. Now how does this help me escape adulthood, you ask? Well, two ways, 1) by helping me overcome the fear of the unknown I had about going to the doctor (Going to the doctor will help me get back to doing some of the fun childlike things I enjoy like playing softball this summer.); And 2) looking at the cool photos and illustrations was a neat way to indulge the curious scientist in me!

Challenge #30:

Funjection Device

The thing that stinks about Adulthood is how many stupid things we have to do. Things we *hate* to do. Wasn't Adulthood supposed to be a mecca of freedom? Free from the iron will of our parents, we were supposed to live life on our terms: stay up late, eat dessert first, abstain from chores we disliked. Adulthood is not all it was cracked up to be. It's true, our lives are filled with some mundane – even hated – chores that are our responsibility. But that doesn't mean we can't inject a little fun.

The Challenge: Figure out a way to bring some fun into a dreaded task today.

Kim:

My dreaded task…two words: cold calls. How in the world do I make cold calls more fun? Well, the first thing I did was I taped an artificial flower (my favorite — the daisy) to the end of my pen. This added some fun to the notes I wrote throughout my calls. I also made up a little game in which I kept track of what types of calls I had. I took a long strip of paper and drew a line down the middle. It was a race. For every good call, I drew a heart in the happy row. For every bad call, I drew a heart in the sad row. I used hearts because of Valentine's Day. It was fun, but I have to say that it wasn't SUPER fun. If anyone has any other ideas on how to make cold calls more fun, please let me know.

Jason:

I am my own boss, so if I had too many "dreaded tasks" littering my schedule, I'd request a one-on-one, closed door meeting with myself. To be honest, I'm not a big fan of the financial side of things; keeping track of all the bills and taxes that need to be paid. But that task was yesterday. Today's agenda consisted of writing and drawing comic strips…not a bad way to spend a day.

But there is one part of my day that I don't particularly look forward to: working out. Maybe it's because I do it first thing in the morning when I still long for sleep; maybe it's because I'm not (yet) as ripped as Toby Maguire in *Spiderman* (hey, don't laugh), but I generally dread this little morning routine. I figured I could put on some music, but that seemed pretty tame. I decided to pop in my *Star Wars Episode III* DVD and watch one of the special feature documentaries. Now that's the way to go. I watched "The Chosen One," which covers the whole sordid tale of Darth Vader, including the cool makeup used to transform Hayden Christensen into a charred and crispy Anakin Skywalker.

In a related story, after my workout I fried myself an egg.

Sue:

I usually dread brushing my teeth at night – not because it's hard or anything, but I typically am so tired I crawl into bed and completely forget about it. That again happened tonight, but this afternoon I had thought of what I wanted to do for this task, so I hopped right back out of bed, put the toothpaste on the toothbrush and then stepped right into the shower, pj's on, curtain closed, and standing on one foot...and yup, I brushed my teeth in the shower. I'm glad I got back out of bed to do this one.

Ian:

Friday is my work-at-home day, and I was trying to fix a particularly annoying bug that has been sitting on my to-do list for the last six months. I had to keep restarting a server, and then changing things to test it worked correctly and didn't break anything worse than it was to start with. Not particularly fun. And the fact I had managed to put it off for six months is a good indication that I wasn't looking forward to it too much.

I noticed a book sitting on the bookshelf to my left – a book of logic puzzles. The type with a bunch of clues and a grid you use to determine who did what, where and when kind of thing. My mother-in-law found it at her place lying around and gave it to me the other day. Thanks, Carol! So while I was waiting for restarts and tests to run, I solved a few of these puzzles. Not super exciting, but it made me feel a whole lot better.

Jaimie:

I wouldn't say this is a most dreaded task (I grocery shopped and looked at the budget yesterday), but I get a wee bit tired of cleaning the high chair tray. I think it's the sheer number of times that it's done day in and day out. So before I washed away the oatmeal and applesauce this morning, I popped in a lovely CD I made for myself entitled "Cardinal Bar." Yep, "Stayin' Alive" was heard over the running water…

Challenge #31:

Listen Up

Scientists have said that the number of places on Earth where a person can go to experience complete and utter quiet is dwindling fast. Our lives have become blanketed by the white noise of rush hour traffic, the beats flowing from our iPods, and thousands of daily invasive mass marketing messages. Our world is noisy. And yet have you ever stopped – really stopped – to actually *listen*? You may be surprised by what you hear.

The Challenge: Find a place to sit quietly for ten minutes. Listen for at least one sound that you would not have normally noticed.

Kim:

I decided to sit on a bench in a nearby park which overlooks an open field. It is a very peaceful place. I've gone there before to sit, but this time was very different, it was sans my iPod. There were many obvious sounds: cars driving by, the far-off sound of vehicles on the highway, birds, dogs barking, more dogs, more birds, more cars… then I heard it: the THUMP of a basketball against the backboard. THUMP. It was very faint and seemed to be far away, but it was a very distinct sound and upon hearing it, I was immediately whisked back to my driveway growing up on Shady Lane. All of the games of PIG and HORSE…all of the missed shots. That sound was very familiar to me. It's funny, had I heard the "swoosh," I don't think I would've been "whisked back."

Jason:

I like going on walks. In my estimation, running is only good for those times when you're being chased by a puma. But pumas are pretty fast, so even then, it comes up useless.

Anyway, I usually take a walk in the morning, and there is a little park in the neighborhood behind our place. I decided to sit there for a while. At first, I could only hear the annoying din of "worldly" sounds: the hum of distant city traffic, a jet flying overhead, a garbage truck making its rounds. Eventually, I started to notice the squirrels playing in the brush nearby. And then I heard the birds. In the beginning, there was only one generic "bird" sound, but it wasn't long before I could start to make out different species. Three, maybe four unique bird calls arranged themselves in a chorus that heralded the coming of spring.

It reminded me of how easy it is to get caught up in the world, in the stresses of life. But if we can sit our butts down for ten minutes, a whole new world emerges right from under us. The happy songs of the birds gave me a feeling of peace, and reminded me of the time when Jesus said:

> "Therefore I tell you, do not worry about your life…Consider the birds: They do not sow or reap, they have no storeroom or barn; yet God feeds them. And how much more valuable you are than birds! Who of you by worrying can add a single hour to his life? Since you cannot do this very little thing, why do you worry about the rest?" (Luke 12:22-26)

The birds *did* seem pretty happy about things, and as much as I enjoy walking, I was happy that I took the time to just sit.

- -

Sue:

I went outside behind an office building I was working at near the highway, so the most predominant sound was cars going by. I sat in the gazebo behind the building to see if I could hear anything else. I heard dry leaves being blown by the wind, both those still on trees and those on the ground. Hard to believe that in February there are dried leaves on the ground in Wisconsin, but I digress. Paper was blowing behind me through the crackling leaves, but then I got up to walk and I heard more sounds: a motorcycle from another direction, a truck's diesel engine, footsteps on pavement. But then I stopped and listened, and heard a very faint clanking, but I couldn't tell where it was coming from. The wind was too strong for it to be the flagpole that was on the other side of another building. Then I went closer to the lamppost and leaned my ear up against it. Sure enough, there was a cable inside rattling around – it did sound like a flag rope as it hits its pole. This was a very fascinating experience! I think I'll have to try it again sometime.

Jenna:

I took my ten minute silent time at the mall. I found a bench in one of the center areas and concentrated on listening to all the levels of sounds: people walking and talking, chimes sounding as people entered stores, strollers rolling along, kids laughing/crying/yelling. I also heard a humming noise which I believe was the heating system, a jangling of keys as the mall cop strolled by and then, then I heard whistling. It wasn't a tune I was familiar with, but it was a very pretty melody. I waited and looked around until I spotted him: a custodial serviceman. He was probably 60 years old or so, pushing along his cart and whistling away, a smile on his face. He reminded me of my grandfather who used to whistle while he took his walks and also when he was down in his workshop.

Walt:

Last Saturday, I was invited to my son Jason's surprise birthday party. My middle son and his wife were in the middle of having their third child, so Linda and I took the two girls with us to the party. We all had a blast, the old and the young, the old friends and new friends. It really made for a special day. We stayed way longer than I thought we would. After the party, we had a 75-minute ride back to the girls' home in the family minivan. We were about halfway home when I heard this unfamiliar sound coming from the back of the van. It was 3-1/2 year old, Kerrigan, snoring. Now kids don't snore like us big folks. We have it down to a gross body function – you all know what I mean. The ones that are really bad are when a person takes a deep breath and then silence. Or the snore that sounds like someone just buried their nose in pudding, you know all that spoot sound inside.

But kids have that soft snore that sounds peaceful. I think I saw some z's floating towards the front of the van.

Laugh Attack

Ever notice how much four-year-olds seem to enjoy life? It has been said that the average preschooler laughs about 400 times a day. The average grown-up clocks in at about, oh, 15 or so laughs per day. We don't know about you, but for some of the people we know, even that number seems high. Clearly, we've fallen off the wagon and we need help. We need to laugh way more than we do. It's good for us, and if you do it right, it keeps the manufacturers of laundry detergent in business.

The Challenge: Do something that will get you to laugh out loud (one that puts you in danger of peeing your pants a little bit).

Kim:

I love stand-up comedy. It started when I was younger watching Bill Cosby, Paula Poundstone, Tim Allen, Jerry Seinfeld, Jeff Foxworthy and Ellen Degeneres – before she was known as just "Ellen." I tend to laugh out loud quite a bit at stand-up comedy. So, knowing this, I put on some Dane Cook, which we had in iTunes, while I was doing some busywork this morning. Dane is unbelievably funny. Sure enough, within minutes I was cracking up. Sometimes I think I laugh harder at the jokes I already know because I'm anticipating the funny parts that are coming up. Why don't I do this more? I know what makes me laugh, yet I would never have normally put on comedy during the day. It really got me in a great mood.

Jason:

When I need a laugh fix, I like watching funny movies — the kind my mom thinks are stupid (but secretly laughs at too). Because I didn't have time to watch a full movie, I browsed some of the best parts of my favorite ones, compliments of MovieWavs.com. Here are some highlights:

Anchorman
Ron: "What cologne are you gonna go with? London Gentlemen, or — wait. No, no, no. Hold on. Blackbeard's Delight."
Brian: "No, she gets a special cologne. It's called Sex Panther by Odeon. It's illegal in nine countries. Yep, it's made with bits of real panther. So you know it's good."
Ron: "It's quite pungent."
Brian: "Oh yeah."
Ron: "Ooh, it's a formidable scent. It stings the nostrils. In a good way."
Brian: "Yeah."
Ron: "Brian, I'm gonna be honest with you. That smells like pure gasoline."

National Lampoon's Christmas Vacation
Eddie: "Yeah, I got the daughter in the clinic, getting cured off the Wild Turkey. And, the older boy, bless his soul, is preparing for his career."
Clark: "College?"
Eddie: "Carnival."
Clark: "You got to be proud."
Eddie: "Oh, yeah. Yeah, last season he was a pixie-dust spreader on the Tilt-O-Whirl. He thinks that maybe next year, he'll be guessing people's weight or barking for the Yak woman. You ever see her?"
Clark: "No."
Eddie: "She's got these big horns growing right out above her ears. Yeah, she's ugly as sin, but a sweet gal. And, a hell of a good cook."

Napoleon Dynamite
Don (Trevor Snarr): "Hey, Napoleon, what'd you do all last summer again?"
Napoleon: "I told you! I spent it with my uncle in Alaska hunting wolverines!"

Don: "Did you shoot any?"

Napoleon: "Yes, like 50 of 'em! They kept trying to attack my cousins. What the heck would you do in a situation like that?"

Don: "What kind of gun did you use?"

Napoleon: "A frickin' 12-gauge, what do you think?"

- -

Doug and Katie:

While in the dollar store picking up oversized clown sunglasses, Katie had the great idea of trying to drive with them on! It was quite funny to both of us. Strangely, no one on the road really seemed to notice. It made us laugh out loud and still does. Plus, living with a comedian, we laugh out loud every day!

Marci:

We got Dad an iPod for his birthday last week; I was at Mom and Dad's this afternoon. Dad had his iPod, singing along as loud as he could (and quite off key and making up his own lyrics as he listened). He was having so much fun, but his "singing/songwriting" got me rolling with laughter, and I did almost pee in my pants!

Ian:

On the train on the way home, I had a small boy (maybe 6) and his mother sit opposite me in a 4-seater. The young boy was getting a bit bored, as I was doing a crossword and his mum was just sitting there. She didn't look much older than me. Anyway, I put my crossword away and just sat there pulling subtle faces at him. He decided that it was appropriate to do the "underarm fart" trick. Repeatedly.

My response was probably the best (for him) and the worst (for his mum, trying to remain serious on a packed train) – I tried not to laugh. Of course, this resulted in me cracking up and laughing long and loud along with him.

I thought about joining in myself, but I have never learned the art of the underarm fart.

Challenge #33:
Spoiled Rotten

We believe that one of the primary roles of grandparents is to spoil their grandchildren. If all goes according to plan, parents should keep a pretty tight ship, which allows Grandma and Grandpa to swoop in on occasion and offer the grandkids a respite of giddy indulgence. The way we see it, that's the reward grandparents get for doing a good job with their own kids. Even if you've never had the privilege of this sort of special relationship, a good childhood has just the right amount of these flashes of superfluousness. Think Halloween and birthday parties.

The Challenge: For no reason at all, treat yourself to something out of the ordinary.

Kim:
My treat involved Jason's face. Yes, the surprised look on his face when he walked through the door into his 30th (surprise!) birthday party. There is nothing more thrilling than the 30 seconds before the guest of honor comes into the surprise party and the 30 seconds after he/she has arrived. The biggest treat of all, though, was when I asked him if he knew about it, hoping he hadn't been pretending for my sake, and he honestly assured me that he didn't know. Woo hoo!

Jason:
My version of an out-of-the-ordinary treat was completely overshadowed about fifteen minutes after I finished the challenge. I had lunch today with my brother Doug, and afterwards I had to

run to the grocery store to pick up some mushrooms for Kim. I decided to splurge and pick up a pint of Ben & Jerry's® ice cream (Cherry Garcia®). Definitely a treat in our household. The fact that it was on sale made me think it was my lucky day…

Then Doug and I made our way back to my place. I opened the door and was overwhelmed by a living room filled with friends and family all yelling "Surprise!" My wife, with the help of some busy beavers, had successfully pulled off a surprise 30th birthday party for me. I was blown away. I didn't suspect a thing. It was really, really cool. I got a chance to spend time with my best friends, and reconnect with others that I hadn't seen in a while. (By the way, if you're wondering what kind of gifts a 30-year-old cartoonist with a specialty in escaping adulthood gets for his birthday, let's just say I got more toys than an average nine-year-old. My three-year-old niece was perched by my side, completely jealous.)

And to top it all off, near the end of the evening, I got a call from my other brother Dan informing me that his wife had just delivered a 9-pound baby boy. So I guess that makes me an uncle. This definitely ranks right up there on the list of my all-time out-of-the-ordinary days!

- -

Jenna:

My treat included my secret addiction to video games. While cruising the clearance aisles at one of the local discount stores, I spotted a sweet indulgence: one of those plug-into-the-front-of-the-tv video games. It was a super flashback: Intellivision – yes, *Intellivision*. While most of my peers had Atari or even Commodore 64, we had an Intellivision. It had some really fun games including Baseball, Shark! Shark! and my favorite, Burgertime! I found this retro cool game with 10 games from the original game console including Night Stalker and Astrosmash! What a treat!

Jaimie:

I really like reading James Patterson novels for fun (if you've ever read one, you would agree that they have NOTHING to do with my work!). and haven't read one in quite some time. Before heading home for the day, I stopped at the library and picked up a couple in the Detective Alex Cross series. With my hot cocoa in hand, I'm ready to get back to reading – I'm already on page 66.

Walt:

In Peru, Illinois, we have this old time men's clothing store that has been passed down over the years called Vlastnik's Menswear. The younger generation runs the place, and they do a great job. They handle many of the hard-to-find sizes. Today I went in there after work and asked to see their selection of bow ties. The older gentleman looked at me in surprise, and he said they had a box of them some-where. They looked around and then he pulled out this shoe box full of bow ties! I picked out a rather large one, goldish in color and soft, almost like teddy bear material. $5.00. Then I got another about 1/2 the size of the first one. $2.50. I actually did have a blue and white bow tie in my adult years, but have misplaced it and have not seen it for years.

The bow tie has a special place for me because my old boss Peter G. used to wear them all the time. Peter sitting on boxes of Maze Nails became the company trademark. So for around eight bucks, I made myself happy and made the clothing store guys smile!

Challenge #34:
Time Traveler

One of the quickest and simplest ways to get yourself back into a childhood state of mind is to actually do something you used to do as a child. Perhaps it's visiting a meaningful place, humming a long-lost tune, or playing a much-loved game. Give yourself permission to go back in time, and before you know it, that inner child will be awake and jumping for joy.

The Challenge: Think about some of the things you liked to do as a child. Pick one and do it.

Kim:

When I was little, I loved hearing bedtime stories. This was a nightly tradition. Tonight I had the chance to read my two nieces a bedtime story. I squeezed my long legs into the bottom bunk of their bunk bed, and the two exhausted girls, one on each side of me, shared one pillow. They picked out "Berenstain Bears, The Bad Habit." Reading about "Sister Bear" and "Brother Bear" brought back some great memories. That's definitely something I miss about teaching kindergarten — the stories.

Jason:

Today was a long day. After yesterday's whirlwind, we went down to see my brother and his wife and my new nephew, Caden. My blast from the past came during the Super Bowl when my niece offered me a stick of gum. I can't remember the last time I had gum that wasn't spearmint or peppermint flavored — you know, the grown-up flavors. She had three different kinds; I chose grape. A few chews in and I was a kid again, smacking on some Big League Chew. I loved that stuff. It reminded me of sitting on the bench in Little League, cheering for my teammates while pretending to be a big leaguer. It's amazing how your taste buds can conjure up such specific memories.

What's also amazing is how quickly the flavor evaporates after only a few minutes of chewing. All these years later, and still we are a society without long-lasting grape flavored bubble gum.

- -

Jaimie:

When I was of Brownie age, I learned how to braid hair. I really enjoyed it and wanted to practice every chance I got. My younger sister wasn't too into that idea, so I practiced on myself. To this day, I'm much better at braiding my own hair than anybody else's. My hair is not that long now, so I made two short french braids in my hair today. I have a feeling these suited me better in my Brownie days.

Sue:

For this one, all sorts of ideas ran through my head: go shoot hoops and practice my free throws, go swing, play in a sandbox, play with toy tractors, and help my dad with farm chores. I couldn't quite do any of them in the winter time in Wisconsin when I was working 'til way after dark. So I thought of another idea. I used to love it when on very rare occasions, mom or dad would buy a 16 oz. glass bottle of Pepsi®. Just the sound of the bottle being opened (fizz), the feel of glass on the lips (cool), the feeling of the curves on the bottle and the old red and blue Pepsi label. Now, all that being said, they're a little harder to come by these days. But I was able to find the 8 oz. bottles of Coke® (that'll work, especially since my younger sister and I always had to split a 16 oz. one). I got home, broke out the bottle opener (when was the last time I used that?), heard the fizz, and took a big drink. Ahh - the memories!

Marci:

I loved to read when I was younger (actually, I still do). One of my favorite series when I was in middle school and junior high was "The Babysitter's Club." I pulled out one of the books from a box in my parents' basement and started reading it tonight. You know what? I still enjoy the stories!

Ian:

I've always loved the idea of superheroes: people with superhuman abilities fighting crime and all that sort of thing. The idea of being able to do things that mere mortals could not is an idea that I constantly think about. Which abilities would be the best fit for me, and what would my weaknesses be? Telekinesis sounds pretty cool, but laser eyes and adamantium claws are also extremely awesome.

As you can probably guess, as a child I loved watching superhero cartoons, primarily *X-Men*, which was just so well done. I can see flaws in it now that I'm older, but the fact that they killed off (supposedly) one of the main characters – who was even in the opening credits – sealed the deal with me. This wasn't a cartoon like the others I've seen. Also, they got the voices so perfectly right that even seeing live actors play the roles still sounds wrong in my head. Wolverine especially – that guy just didn't put a word wrong, bub.

The comics are cool too. I think my favourite story (having only read the synopsis) is this one in Ultimate X-Men (they started afresh without all the baggage from the hundreds of other comics). A child has recently manifested his mutant ability, the ability to kill all living things that come near him. Wolverine finds him alone in a cave and talks to him, his mutant healing factor keeping him alive near this deadly kid. Ah, just reading that overview makes me feel tingly, it is so well written, and such a sad story. I nearly cried just reading it.

Anyway, after thinking about how cool those comics and cartoons were when I was a kid (and now), I watched a few episodes of *X-Men: Evolution*, the latest cartoon incarnation of these superheroes. Not quite as great as the old cartoons – the new intro music isn't anywhere near as memorable and the voices don't quite fit – but still very well done, with some great stories.

Challenge #35:
Hero For A Day

When it comes right down to it, didn't we all have some semblance of heroic aspirations when we were little? Be it a princess, a superhero, or a firefighter, we all had the urge to be great and make a difference. One thing we often take for granted about adulthood is that we now have many more powers than we ever had as kids to actually make a difference. What could only exist in the imagination of a child with no driver's license, no money, and no freedom to come and go as he pleased; we now have the opportunity to make real. The other thing we forget about is that there is a new generation of kids searching for heroes to look up to.

The Challenge: Do something to make the day of a child.

Kim:
One of the greatest gifts I've received as a teacher has been the relationships I've maintained with some of my former students. I know it makes my day when I get a letter or e-mail from one of my students, telling me what's new and telling me about how big they are now. So today I decided to send some messages to a few of them. When I was little, I had a pen pal, and the days I would receive a letter would truly make my day. It felt really good to send my messages today. I even sent some pictures along.

Jason:
If it were a summer day, I'd try and track down a neighborhood lemonade stand and leave a really big tip. As far as I know, Kim & Jason are the only ones I can think of that would set up shop in the middle of winter in Wisconsin. My thoughts drifted across continents, to a boy named Hailemariam who lives in Ethiopia. Kim and I have been sponsoring "Hal" for about 10 years now through Compassion® International. Through letters and pictures, we've seen him sprout like a weed and become more and more successful in school. My favorite parts of our correspondence have been the little drawings that he'd include with his letters. It has been neat to track his progress through his sketches. At the end of his letters, he always asks for more pictures of us.

We have sent him a lot of snapshots over the years, but I've never done a custom drawing just for him. Today I whipped out the colored pencils and drew Kim, Jason, and Hal sitting together on a brontosaurus. I'll add it to our next letter to him. I can't be certain that it'll make his day, but at least it'll let him know that there's somebody an ocean away thinking of him.

Jaimie:

Since I have a child, you'd think this challenge would be easy for me. I still haven't figured out exactly how to make her day – she's a little on the quiet side. But I read her lots of books, gave her tickles and even let her roam around to meet and greet her fans while out at lunch.

But I think I made the day of a much bigger kid today. We are expecting Baby #2 and my husband was dying to find out the sex of the baby (I'd rather be surprised after all the hard work of labor). In the end, we had an ultrasound yesterday and my husband punched two fists in the air and screamed "yes!" when the technician pointed out something between the legs.

Walt:

Tonight Linda and I decided to get a good start on our granddaughters' presents for Valentine's Day, and what better place to go than Frank's Cigar Store (see my post for Challenge #23). Since the girls have a new baby brother, we had to buy them blue bubble gum "It's a Boy" cigars. We also purchased the following:

Bubble gum beads and crunchy candy watches.
Red Hot Dollars.
Wax Lips (cherry flavored, Jason!)
Cherry dip and lick lollipops.
And the newest rage: Air Heads Xtremes Sour Belts.
I hope this stuff doesn't smell like cigars and please don't tell the girls what we got them!

Carlo:

Inspired by Kim and Jason, my wife and I decided to sponsor a child through the same Compassion.com organization that they use to sponsor Hailemariam in Ethiopia. The dilemma was picking a child. I went on the Compassion.com website and seeing all those children in need broke my heart (who says Republicans don't have hearts?). I e-mailed Kim for advice, and she just happened to have a packet to sponsor a little girl from Bolivia with her at her apartment. I am a big believer in fate and the decision was made. I contacted the people at Compassion to confirm that Mireya had not yet been sponsored, and I was very glad to hear that she was still available. I immediately signed myself and my wife Darlene up as Mireya's sponsors and I now have the anticipation of a five-year-old on Christmas morning waiting for the packet to arrive. I look forward to getting Mireya's photo and information so that we may begin to make a difference in the life of one little girl in Bolivia. Thanks, K & J!

Jenna:

Sometimes completing these challenges take hours of brainstorming and complex planning; other times, opportunities to complete these challenges just show up. Today was a "just show up" day. I am out of town on a sales trip, and I was making a visit to one of the bookstores that carry our book. I was pretty early, and as I was waiting for my contact to finish what she was doing, I wandered around and ended up in the children's section. I found a spot in a little reading corner and grabbed a copy of "CLICK, CLACK, MOO!" (Great book by the way!) As I was getting into the story, a little boy, probably about four or so, came up to look at the book. As I looked him in the eye, he asked, "Canyoureadit-tome?" I said, "Sure" and spent the next five minutes reading about cows that type. His mom came to collect him, apologizing for him bothering me. I told her I was happy to read the story for him. He grinned and waved as she led him away. It made me feel very good to earn that grin in such a simple way.

#

A blue tank top. Polka dot boxer shorts. Knee pads. An orange bow tie. And cowboy boots. When left to their own devices, a child's wardrobe can resemble the leftovers at a garage sale. Kim used to aggravate her mom by changing outfits several times in one day. If he was allowed, Jason would have worn his Yoda costume to church. Please don't think we're about to advocate you pick out an outfit that makes it look like your closet threw up on you. But why not let a little bit of childhood sneak into what you wear today?

The Challenge: Accessorize your wardrobe today with a touch of childhood.

Kim:

When I was in third grade I got my ears pierced. This was a big deal. I was so excited. I had an earring tree, which was home to my many different pairs, both plastic and metal. Now, some twenty years later, I find myself earring-less. I don't often wear them, and I'm not really sure why. So today I dug out my pair of ladybug earrings and put them on. I love them because they really look like I have ladybugs on my earlobes. I think I want to go get a bunch of other childlike earrings. It added a touch of fun to my day. Plus, it was kind of like a warning signal for others who saw me today. WARNING: This person does NOT take herself too seriously (at least I'm trying not to).

Jason:

Today's challenge was a little bit more difficult than it may seem. On any given day, you might find me wearing jeans and a Reese's® Peanut Butter Cup t-shirt. Accessorizing my wardrobe with a touch of

childhood is fairly commonplace for me. Digging a little deeper, I thought about how kids love to play dress-up; getting all spiffed up like a "grown-up" (funny how growing up holds such appeal when you're little). I decided to don dress clothes today, accessorized by a Loony Toons® tie and Superman watch. The only thing missing was my mom's stern warning not to get "all messed up."

Jenna:

For today's challenge I was still on the road, so I only had what I had packed. During my first sales visit I saw the perfect accessory for a childlike touch to my wardrobe – a Ring Pop! It was fun to wear and sweet to eat throughout the day! It got laughs and comments from the store owners I visited today – totally in line with the Kim & Jason mission!

Walt:

Our employees and our customers at Maze Lumber did not realize it, but today was Bow Tie Day! As stated in Challenge #33, I purchased two bow ties at a local men's clothing store. This morning, I stood in front of the bathroom mirror and I clipped on the large gold bow tie. I snapped it into its place and boy, did that bring back childhood memories! I wasn't actually sure if I would wear it all day long especially since I had to go out with our newest salesman to do final measuring of some Marvin® windows. This order would be in the $50,000 range, and I didn't want to make a bad impression. In the end, I decided to just go for it and it was a HUGE success. I think my appearance just tore down the wall of apprehension and it went well. I think that they thought if this guy would wear "that" in public...well whatever.

Back at the shop, the customers had plenty of comments when they spotted the bushy bow tie. It put everyone in a playful mood. My boss Pete – whose father, also named Pete, was a champion in the bow tie movement – was especially entertained by the wardrobe addition to the bright yellow shirts we usually wear. I also think that some of our regular customers thought either I was nuts or gutsy.

In the afternoon, I brought the other smaller bow tie for Pete to don. The general feeling was that mine was Austin Powers-like (which I take as a compliment) and Pete's was Chippendale-like and could fit right in with Chris Farley on that Saturday Night Live skit.

Our new gal Patty said she had some old ties that her mom was going to make into a quilt but never did and I said bring them in. I actually think I will make it a practice to wear either an interesting tie or bow tie once a week. It sure did lighten up the office today!

Ian:

My normal work attire consists of a t-shirt (or normal shirt) and pants. Not exactly standard business attire and the exact type of clothes I wore as a kid. The clothes I wear are pretty much straight from my childhood as it is, so I wasn't sure what I would do for this task.

Until I visited my parents' house.

I found a handbag my mum had made, and saw that if I put it on my head, it looked like a cross between a chef's hat, one of those Russian hats, and a beefeater hat. Cool.

I marched around their house for a bit while wearing it, and managed to get everyone there to laugh out loud. Especially Mat. He fell over laughing.

Kids can wear anything they want and as long as they feel like it's cool, it's cool.

I'm cool.

Tastes Like Childhood

Again, the concept of rekindling your childlike spirit by doing something you actually did regularly as a child cannot be overstated. It's a foolproof way to keep Adultitis at bay. Food is a good way to accelerate the process. We all have favorite things that Mom or Grandma used to make. Or a special treat that dad used to reward us for a job well done (or more likely, a job done halfway decently). Today's your chance to dig up that old recipe card or head to the candy store.

The Challenge: Eat or drink something today that brings back childhood memories.

Kim:

Two words: Swedish Fish! They were like the Cadillac of gummy candy growing up. We rarely got them but when we did, I savored every bite. I honestly haven't had them since childhood, and I'm ashamed that I have deprived myself of such joy all of these years. I have to admit what I was originally looking for was shoestring red licorice. I thought that was so neat that you could tie it in a bow and then eat it. Since we are in a different state tonight

(sunny Florida), I wasn't sure where to even start to shop around. The Swedish Fish were a great second choice. Boy, do they get stuck in your teeth, though...

Jason:

I strolled down the candy aisle at a supermarket in Tampa looking for a package of childhood memories. I found them in a box of Sour Patch Kids. As a wee lad, I loved those little buggers. Most grownups I knew didn't know why I'd subject myself to such a horrible abomination disguised as candy. Sour Patch Kids truly are an assault on the ol' taste buds, and I couldn't get enough of 'em as a kid. It's been a long time since I've had one, but they still make me pucker.

Jenna:

This challenge was an easy one for me; I had a lot of ideas of meals, snacks and beverages that bring back memories from childhood. I finally settled on the classic combination of food and drink: the root beer float! I can remember getting root beer floats as a treat at my grandparents' house. I love the way the vanilla ice cream would get icy on the edges where the root beer would freeze to it. We of course had spoons, and Grandma always had bendy straws too! There is something special about a homemade float! Yum!

Carlo:

Ok, I'll admit that I am not doing these in order. I still have a lot of catching up to do. But I had to participate in this one. I took a very different approach. When I was sick as a child my mom always had the cure, Pepto-Bismol® and 7-UP®. Even though I'm not even sick, I took some Pepto-Bismol and had a 7-UP. Definitely brought back some memories.

Walt:

Swedish Fish and Sour Patch Kids. Cute, but I went in a different direction. Please refer to Challenge #15. Tonight, Linda and I went for supper at the Igloo Restaurant in Peru. This area favorite has been around forever and is known for its pork tenderloins, fries and chili. At first I told Linda that I would have a taste of her chili, but then I thought that was wimpy. I decided to order my own (a cup, not a bowl). Linda said if I didn't eat it all I could expect to have the rest cold for breakfast tomorrow! I ordered this simmering sensation and when it was set in front of me, I did an extreme journey to my early days...chili every other Saturday supper and most Sunday breakfasts. I couldn't believe all the beans and I promised Linda a night of mousies (Kim's childhood name for fart). I figured it's been about 40 years since I stuck a spoon into chili, and I am happy to report that I survived to write this challenge.

Interesting side note was the waitress coming up to us and asking us, "How's the chili?" I asked Linda if she had anything to do with this. But she said, "No."

So there, Virginia (mom), I finally did it! I ate a cup of chili at one sitting. Amen.

Paste Is Not A Food Group

Kids specialize in creating MacGyver-like expressions of love made out of finger paint, paste, and a handful of stale macaroni. Part of it is because they're naturally creative, part of it is because they don't have a bank account that allows them to go out and buy a posh gift basket. And let's face it: the gift basket route is way easier. Creating something from scratch takes more thought, not to mention more time. But when it comes to acknowledging someone you really care about, isn't that really the way to go?

The Challenge: Make someone a homemade gift to show how much you care about him/her or to thank him/her for a job well done.

Kim:

Well, as you may remember from Challenge #33 last Saturday, I hosted a surprise birthday party for Jason to celebrate his 30th birthday, which happens to be *this* Saturday. This party would NOT have happened if it weren't for my sister-in-law, Katie, who initiated the idea and pretty much organized most of it. In order to show her how much I appreciated her help, I took a page out of my own childhood – I made her a homemade card. Ironically, she had brought Jason and I the funny pages a while back from her massive Sunday paper. I had them in the recycling bag, so I dug them out and started reading some of the captions. I ended up cutting out captions and putting them in an order to tell the story of how the party came to be. I even found a cartoon of a little blue bird, which is symbolic for Jason (Jbird). The text came together perfectly. I added some fancy little borders on the card and away it will go to her house. I plan to mail it so she will be surprised, unless of course she reads this first.

Jason:

I hate origami. I only wish I knew that before I started this challenge. I spent half an hour trying to make some "simple" origami creations for Kim. We just got back from Tampa, and she manages all of the details for my speaking engagements. I wanted to thank her for all of her hard work — she really does a great job, and makes it look easy. I was so excited to make a little origami sculpture. "This will be so cool," I thought. "Very creative," I thought. "And simple, too!" I thought.

I blew 15 minutes trying to make a bluebird. I wanted to make a bird because "Jbird" is one of Kim's nicknames for me. Got to about step 6, then the instructions got confusing. I've never been very good at comparing and following 2-D diagrams and 3-D reality (I have a heckuva time putting office furniture together).

Then I decided to try something a bit easier. I found a simple heart project that involved six steps and was supposed to take 1-3 minutes. Ten minutes later and I was ready to throw my origami rejects out the window. Finally, I decided to express my appreciation the old fashioned way: marker on paper. My final project was not as exciting as I had hoped, but at least it was sincere. And frustrating.

(In a related story, while Kim was doing her project — completely independent of me — she found a cartoon of A BLUEBIRD MAKING ORIGAMI. I wish I could make this stuff up.)

Marci:

Tonight, I'm making a "friendship bracelet" to send to my friend Robin in San Francisco. Some of you might remember them…a very popular craft for girls (and boys) who grew up in the 80's. I still remember the knot-y technique, yet it's been some 15 years since I last made one. I hope Robin likes it!

Jenna:

Tonight I baked some cookies from a favorite family recipe – Cowboy Cookies! There are a lot of memories wrapped up in the smell of chocolate and oatmeal fresh from the oven – YUMMY! They will be a gift for friends of mine who have asked me to be the godmother to their second child. I am grateful for the honor.

Sue:

I pulled out the construction paper, crayons, and colored pencils and made a homemade "thank you" Valentine's Day card for my mom and dad. My mom is the champion of writing – she writes all five of us kids weekly (or pretty close to it). But do I write back? Rarely! I can probably count on one hand how many times I have. I usually pick up the phone and call, which is good, but it would be nice for them to receive a little surprise in the mail too. So I did that. I hope they will get it on Valentine's Day and know how much I love them and appreciate all they have done and continue to do for me.

Challenge #39:

Court Jester

Be it a knock-knock joke or the classic "pull a quarter from my ear" gag, kids love a good ruse. This challenge attempts to coax from you a little of that mischievous and impish spirit. From the giddy anticipation to the joyous reveal, nothing beats a good, harmless practical joke.

The Challenge: Play a practical joke on someone.

Kim:

As I was thinking about this challenge in the shower this morning, the perfect idea fell from the sky (or at least from over the shower curtain). As part of Jason's practical joke on me, he threw marshmallows over the curtain at me. I was not expecting that at all. This did inspire me to seek revenge as the motivation for the practical joke I would soon play on him. As more marshmallows showed up throughout the day, I was more and more excited to get to lunch where my joke would take place. I decided to take one of the many marshmallows that Jason threw at me and I hide it at the bottom of his cup of milk. In order to get it heavy enough to keep it at the bottom of the cup, I stuffed the marble from Challenge #5 in the center, along with about six pennies. Jason drank almost all of his milk until he got to the very end and saw the nasty mushy marshmallow at the bottom. He was pretty surprised and grossed out.

Jason:

I'm not a practical joker by nature, and I'm not especially fond of the really cruel ones (maybe I'm afraid of karma exacting revenge). It took me a while to get into the spirit, but once I did, I had fun with it. I took a playful approach on my target, who happened to be some girl named Kim.

I marshmallowed her.

We had a stale bag of jumbo marshmallows in the cupboard, so I decided to put them to good use. I threw a couple into her shower this morning. I hid some in her shoes, her stocking hat, her glove, her purse, the dashboard of the car, and in each of her coat pockets. She's been discovering marshmallows all day long. It was so cool to watch in anticipation as she found each one. And as of this writing, there are even some hiding spots she hasn't found yet. Of a better use for stale marshmallows I cannot think.

Walt:

For me, this was a breeze! For as long as I can remember, I have had the ability to pull off some pretty good practical jokes. One of my favorites was the time I took my boss' solar calculator, and I perfectly cut a piece of electrical tape and placed it over the solar cells. He couldn't figure out why it wouldn't work and even asked one of the "brighter" office guys who couldn't figure it out either. During his lunch hour, Pete went out and bought a new calculator. After lunch, he showed me his new calculator and then explained his old one just quit working. I looked at it and pulled off the black tape and it worked just fine!

Today, I wrote Pete a note saying that his brother Jim from the nail mill called and said he just got word that all employees at both businesses that operate forklifts have to have a refresher course by the end of February to keep their certification valid. Call brother Jim ASAP! Then I called the yard manager in and told him what I had just "learned."

Pete called Jim and asked about the forklift course. Needless to say, Jim was confused and Pete was scratching his head looking at my note. I walked up to Pete and set in front of him this note: "#39. Play a practical joke on someone." Pete then told Jim, "Never mind, I just figured it out." Later, I called the yard manager in and told him it was a hoax, and he called me a horse's something.

Jenna:

Bubble wrap came into play in my practical joke. I put a section of bubble wrap under my roommate's bathroom rug. While she thought that was a weak attempt to "get her," it was a minor distraction for my main prank! When she went to get into bed, I heard the covers pulled back and then…uncontrollable laughter! You see, I had covered her two favorite stuffed animals with plastic wrap! HA! After she told me I "got her good" and unwrapped her friends, she laid back only to find that her pillow had that crinkly noise too – yup, I shrink-wrapped her pillow too! All in all, very fun and funny without being too mean. That was a LOT of fun!

Ian:

I discovered a little trick a while ago: if you click your fingers on both sides of someone's head, the sound seems to come from inside their skull.

This isn't a very amazing practical joke, but you can give people near-heart attacks with it if they don't notice you coming. It's even funnier if there are a bunch of people watching you creep up behind someone in mid-conversation.

I did this at work and nearly killed a guy (sorry, Mark).

It has now become kind of my work trademark, and people see if they can catch me out with it too – they even manage it occasionally.

In other kinda-related news: I once convinced my Nana I was a carpet steam-cleaning salesman and had her on the phone for fifteen minutes trying to convince me that she didn't need her carpet cleaned.

Sorry, Nana.

Challenge #40:

Sick Of It Day

Well, you did it. Thirty-nine challenges down, one to go. This one's a biggie; a litmus test, if you will. If you've made it this far, and successfully accomplished each challenge, you are on the verge of saying sayonara to Adultitis. Congratulations!

The Challenge: Your final test is to take tomorrow off. Spend today making any necessary adjustments. Do anything you want, but no work and no chores. Consider it a sick day or at least a "sick of it" day (remember, Adultitis is a serious affliction).

Kim:

For us, this challenge fell on February 11th — Jason's 30th birthday. It was also a Saturday. We did have some fun celebrating the occasion, but figured we wouldn't live up to the true spirit of this challenge if we did it on a weekend. So we set Tuesday as our "Sick Of It" day. It's a day we probably shouldn't have taken off because it's a pretty busy week. However, it IS Valentine's Day, and it IS our 11th anniversary of when we started officially dating.

My day started when I rolled out of bed at 10 a.m. One of my guilty pleasures in life is sleeping in. I made a point to turn off the ringers on the phones before we went to bed, so they would not interfere with my plans to snooze later. As I just started to wake up, I turned on the TV and Jason came bouncing in (he heard the TV) and asked if I wanted to be spontaneous. So I put on my Dr. Seuss hat, and off we drove to a neighboring town to get some breakfast at one of our favorite spots. We rarely go out to breakfast, so this was a fun treat. The rest of the day was filled with bumming around town at a couple stores, lunch with a friend, a walk in the long overdue mild weather, a nap, and finally dinner at one of our favorite joints, Outback Steakhouse. Yummy! It was a great day. So many times our weekends end up being injected with paying the bills, laundry, straightening up, etc. It was so nice to have a day to enjoy and relax. I wish my boss would let me do this once a week...

Jason:

Kim did a great job of covering the highlights from the day, so I thought I'd add my random two cents. Most people automatically assume that they could never take a "Sick Of It Day." I think that in most cases, that's a big fat cop-out. What would happen if you came down with a terrible case of pneumonia this evening? Would you be forced to go to work anyway? What if you got seriously injured or — gasp! — killed on your way home from work tomorrow? Would you think to yourself, "Boy, am I sure glad I put in that full day of work today." Don't get me wrong, I'm not advocating a complete and utter disregard for all personal responsibility. I'm talking about ONE day.

To me, the ones who can't get themselves to take a "Sick Of It Day" — I'm talking maybe one or three a year — are only proving that they're not really in control of their life. They let life dictate the terms while they act passively, missing the best of what life has to offer. They're the ones who wake up one day wondering why life didn't treat them better, why it didn't turn out the way they hoped. I heard a speaker — a bishop, in fact — who talked about life being like a stream. You're in a canoe. If you do nothing more than just sit in your canoe, you *will* move. The current *will* take you somewhere. But if you care about *where* you end up, you have to put a little muscle into it. You have to paddle. Sometimes the current will be on your side, and the paddling will be easy. Sometimes you'll be rowing against the current, and your path will be difficult. To me, that's what The Escape Plan is all about: changing the way you think and act. There are a million and one reasons to stay still in that boat. Change is never easy. But if you want to end up somewhere that gives you a feeling of peace, happiness and true fulfillment, it'll take a little effort. One thing that I've learned from this whole thing is that the effort is SO worth it.

Walt:

I hope you had as much fun reading my challenges as I had living them. You two provided the vehicle to go on this journey, and I provided the fuel. And I found out that this vehicle runs on many different types of fuel...some stuff I've never thought possible.

I'd like to know the number of people I affected/infected these last 40 days!

And I want to thank both of you for letting us learn a little bit more about you and sharing your thoughts and the videos. This journey is over, but I have a feeling that there will be more.

Ian:

I actually finished the forty days on (or about) the fortieth day – it's just taken me a while to write them up. My "sick of it" day was a Saturday, so I didn't have any formal work to do anyway (which is good), but our lawn was about three feet high. I decided that I was sick of doing the lawn, and just didn't do it (or the dishwasher, or washing, or any other chores). I tried to get Jen not to do these things either (they could wait a day).

The only real work-type stuff I did was nappy changing. It's a bit of work, but hey, leave that for a day, and you'll really be having problems (plus, a screaming two-year-old is not great for relaxing).

I'm currently on holidays from work (due to baby #2 being born and Jen needing some help), and our lawn needs mowing again. Sick-of-it day take two? I'm not sure. We'll see whether I can avoid mowing for another day.

Thanks, Kim and Jason for the forty days worth of ideas. I know some of them I'll keep doing, and some I'll plan for again. Maybe I'll try and do the whole forty days again in a few years. We'll see.

If you enjoyed this book, you'll love Escape Plan TV. In each episode, Kim and Jason travel to different parts of the world, tackling assorted Escape Plan challenges along the way. The show offers funny, thought-provoking, real-world tips and techniques for living life with less stress and more fun. From California to Florida, from flying kites to kissing giraffes, you won't want to miss any of the action!

www.KimandJason.com/eptv

Kim feeds a giraffe with her mouth in Colorado Springs.

Kim talks about a fun visit to San Francisco's Chinatown.

Jason explains a silly experiment the duo performed in Clearwater, Florida.

The Comic Strip

The *Kim & Jason* comic strip has been published internationally since 2000. Jason Kotecki first drew his lovable characters for his girlfriend Kim while they were dating many years ago. The couple shared a kindred childlike spirit, and Jason used the drawings, which represented the couple as children, on many homemade gifts designed to win her heart. Luckily for him, he not only won her heart, but also her hand in marriage. The characters have since taken on lives of their own and the "real" Kim and Jason have built a company to share the comic strip and its inspiring message. Check out **www.KimandJason.com** for more!

Dark Room Confessional Videos

In addition to writing about their experiences with each challenge on The Escape Plan blog (www.TheEscapePlanBlog.com), Kim and Jason also recorded videos to document their progress. These short clips, featuring more personal insights from the duo, can be found online as well. The first ten are free, and the remaining videos are available to Club K&J subscribers. Find out more about Club K&J at **www.KimandJason.com/clubkj**

Speaking Opportunities

Kim and Jason are professional speakers with the unique ability to connect with audiences of any age. The former school teacher and professional cartoonist are funny and engaging. With hilarious anecdotes, witty observations, and real-world tips, Kim and Jason will entertain and inspire attendees from all walks of life to break free from the stresses of life and become happier, healthier, and more productive. To learn more about bringing them in to speak to your organization, please visit **www.KimandJason.com/speaking.**

Club K&J

People tend to wish you'd take things a little bit more seriously. You wish they'd lighten up and crack a smile once in a while. It's not that you're irresponsible, you just don't need the stress of the fast-paced rat race to find real happiness.

If this sounds a lot like you (or the person you'd like to become, for that matter), welcome home. We saved a space for you as a member of Club K&J. Belong to a playful group of folks who are interested in living life with less stress and more fun. If you have a full-blown or even just a mild case of Adultitis, a yearly subscription is just what the doctor ordered! Here are just some of the benefits...

- A copy of *Escape Adulthood: 8 Secrets from Childhood for the Stressed-Out Grown-Up* AND a nifty members-only t-shirt. (a $30 value)
- An amazing 25% discount on all Kim & Jason Lemonade Stand orders (including shipping!)
- 4 annual issues of the Escape Adulthood magazine, packed with practical tips for living life with less stress and more fun — mailed right to your door. ($32 annual value)
- Automatic entry into the Supremely Wonderful & Exciting Loot Lottery, where we give away things like gourmet jelly beans and concert tickets!
- Every Christmas, you'll receive the annual limited edition Kim & Jason print (a $35 value)
- Plus, $2 of your subscription fee is donated to the Make-A-Wish Foundation®.

All this and more for an annual subscription of only $49.95!
Subscribe today or purchase a Gift Subscription
w w w . K i m a n d J a s o n . c o m / c l u b k j

Escape Plan On-the-Go

This journal was designed to be highly portable, something that you could take along with you on your Escape Plan adventure. But sometimes the journey requires that you pack even lighter, which is why we've included this handy tear-out guide. Just rip it out (it's ok, don't be shy), fold it up, stick it in your purse or pocket, and you'll be able to tackle any challenge at a moment's notice!

☐ **1. Different World.** Spend at least 15 minutes immersing yourself in a field you know nothing about.

☐ **2. Instaparty.** Find a reason to celebrate and do something to celebrate it.

☐ **3. Says You.** Do something that is typically seen as inappropriate for someone of your age.

☐ **4. Souvenir from Childhood.** Add something childlike (not childish) to your workspace or home.

☐ **5. Mad Scientist.** Become a scientist. Conduct a silly experiment.

☐ **6. Daydream Believer.** Write down one big dream of yours. Draw or find a picture to go with it and put it somewhere you will see it often.

☐ **7. Indulge Thyself.** Spend 15 – 30 minutes doing something you love that you don't often have the chance to do.

☐ **8. Doodlesmile.** Draw a funny picture and hide it in an unexpected place for someone else to find.

☐ **9. Rebel With A Cause.** Do one thing today to support a cause or issue you really care about.

☐ **10. Memory Maker.** Create a memory today with someone you care about that will mean a lot ten years from now.

☐ **11. You're Not The Boss of Me.** Do something your parents would never let you do as a child.

☐ **12. Dear Hero.** Write a letter to a childhood hero (real or fictional).

☐ **13. Backyard Adventurer.** Spend ten minutes doing something outside that you have never done before.

☐ **14. Random Act.** Do something to help someone you don't know.

☐ **15. Taste Bud Conspiracy.** Eat something you've never had before.

☐ **16. Family Tree Trivia.** Call or meet with someone in your family and ask them a question you are curious about regarding your family's history.

☐ **17. Old Dog, New Tricks.** Learn how to do something new today. Your time limit: 30 minutes.

☐ **18. Prison Break.** Get out of your element. Go somewhere you've never been before.

☐ **19. Future Forecast.** Spend 10 minutes visioning yourself 10 years from now as having accomplished one of your biggest dreams. Be as detailed as possible; imagine in all five senses.

☐ **20. Instant Karma.** Right an old wrong.

☐ **21. Thanku Haiku.** Write a haiku about the things you are thankful for and put is somewhere to serve as a reminder.

☐ **22. This Little Light of Mine.** Do something to make the world a better place.

☐ **23. Photo Safari.** Take a picture of the most childlike spot in town.

☐ **24. Outside The Lines.** Figure out a way to add some color to your day in a new, unusual, or wacky way.

☐ **25. G'Day Mate.** Talk in a phony voice or accent to a complete stranger.

☐ **26. Mr. Smartypants.** Open to a random page in the dictionary and look at the first word on the upper left-hand side. Keep turning pages until you find a word you don't know. (Or, click on this link for a random word.) See how many times you can use this new word in a sentence today.

☐ **27. Spin Cycle.** Take a routine you do everyday and put a childlike spin on it.

☐ **28. Five Hundred Pennies.** Buy something that captures the spirit of childhood for under $5.00 (including tax).

☐ **29. Just Like George.** Ask an expert something you are curious about in his/her field.

☐ **30. Funjection Device.** Figure out a way to bring some fun into a dreaded task today.

☐ **31. Listen Up.** Find a place to sit quietly for ten minutes. Listen for at least one sound that you would not have normally noticed.

☐ **32. Laugh Attack.** Do something that will get you to laugh out-loud (one that puts you in danger of peeing your pants a little bit).

☐ **33. Spoiled Rotten.** For no reason at all treat yourself to something out of the ordinary.

☐ **34. Time Traveler.** Think about some of the things you liked to do as a child. Pick one and do it.

☐ **35. Hero For A Day.** Do something to make the day of a child.

☐ **36. Dress Up Day.** Accessorize your wardrobe today with a touch of childhood.

☐ **37. Tastes Like Childhood.** Eat or drink something today that brings back childhood memories.

☐ **38. Paste Is Not A Food Group.** Make someone a homemade gift to show how much you care about him/her or to thank him/her for a job well done.

☐ **39. Court Jester.** Play a practical joke on someone.

☐ **40. Sick Of It Day.** Congratulations on making it to the end. Your final test is to take tomorrow off. Spend today making any necessary adjustments. Do anything you want, but no work and no chores. Consider it a sick day or at least a "sick of it" day.